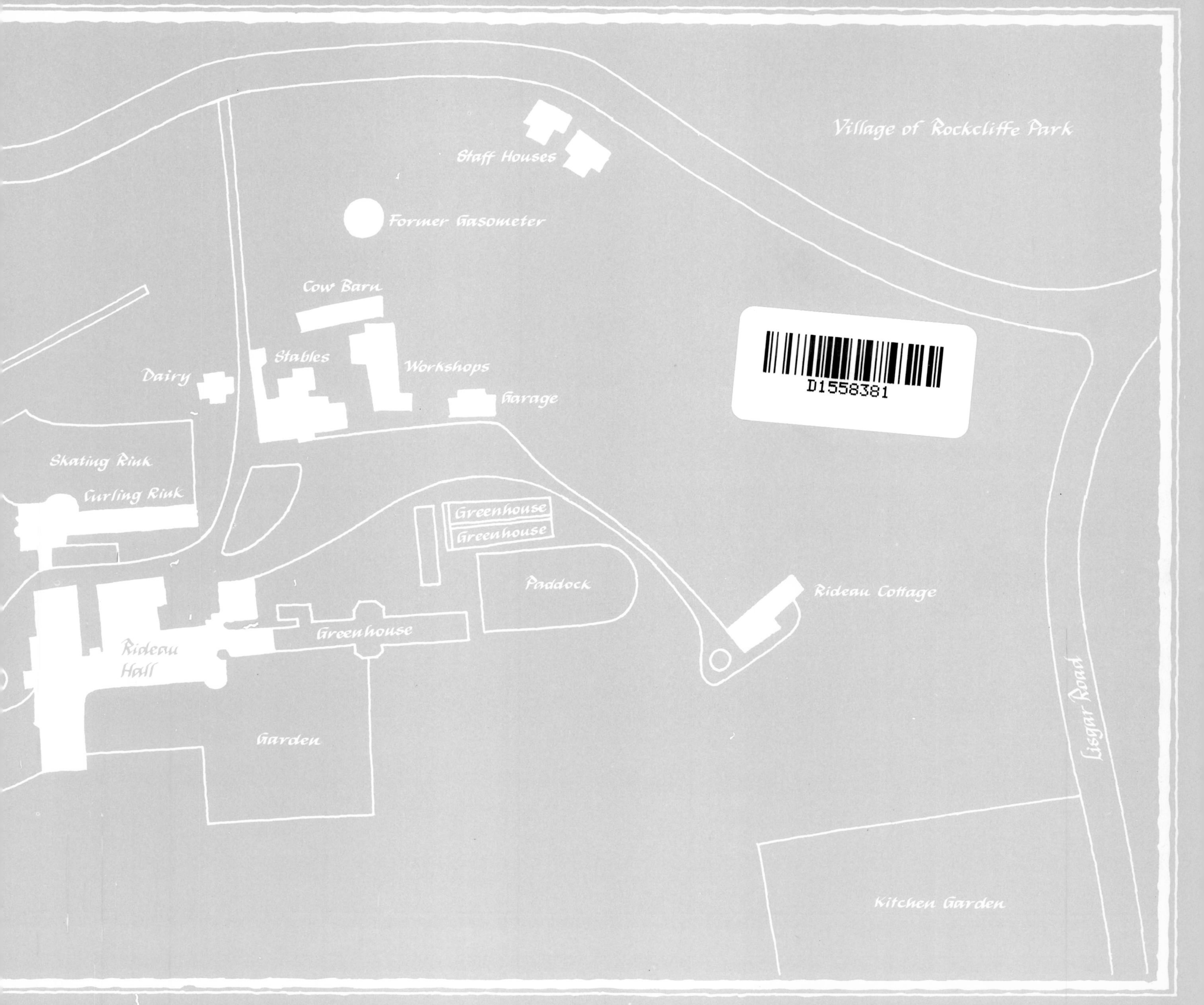

Village of Rockcliffe Park

Staff Houses

Former Gasometer

Cow Barn

Stables

Dairy

Workshops

Garage

Skating Rink

Curling Rink

Greenhouse

Greenhouse

Paddock

Rideau Cottage

Greenhouse

Rideau Hall

Garden

Lisgar Road

Kitchen Garden

D1558381

RIDEAU HALL

RIDEAU HALL

An Illustrated History of Government House, Ottawa

R. H. HUBBARD

Victorian and Edwardian Times

Foreword by His Excellency General The Right Honourable
GEORGES P. VANIER, D.S.O., M.C., C.D.,
Governor-General of Canada

Published by
ROGER DUHAMEL, F.R.S.C.
Queen's Printer and Controller of Stationery
Ottawa, Canada, 1967

To Their Excellencies

The Governor-General of Canada and Madame Vanier

My predecessor, the Right Honourable Vincent Massey, was among the first, if not the first, to recognize the need for a book of this kind. He spoke to me about it when I came to Government House. I thought there might be some difficulty in finding an author because I knew the records available about the early days of Government House and its occupants were scattered and fragmentary. I need not have worried. When I mentioned the matter to Dr Hubbard, his response was enthusiastic.

He proved an intrepid and tireless sleuth. Travelling to Europe, he discovered sources which less patient researchers might not have found. His tact and discretion opened many doors, and indeed many hearts. In the end he was able to assemble much material, the greater part of which had never been made public. So understanding and human are his descriptions that the characters involved come to life with warmth and animation.

The subject-matter of this volume was first presented by Dr Hubbard in a series of talks at the National Gallery. Those fortunate enough to attend them will understand when I say that they were events to which my wife and I looked forward with keen anticipation.

In many ways Government House personifies the nation. Often it is the only Canadian home which some foreign visitors come to know. The House, which is also called Rideau Hall, is not luxurious, nor is it extravagantly appointed, but it is comfortable and reflects much of the charm of the traditional Canadian way of life. Its hospitality, of course, is not confined to foreign visitors; Canadians from all walks of life are welcomed as well.

Past Governors-General, in their quiet way, have exercised an influence on the destiny of the Canadian nation, providing, as they have, wise advice outside of politics and removed from the emotions of day-to-day partisan involvement.

Government House serves on occasion as a neutral meeting ground, a setting where disciples of opposing interests can reconcile and compromise. This neutrality is possible only because the Governor-General is removed from political controversy and, representing as he does the Monarchy, provides the continuity and sense of permanence so valuable in the transient politics of a democracy.

The Governors-General portrayed so vividly by Dr Hubbard were men of ability and wide experience. They brought to Canada an international perspective which was of great value to the young nation.

This book, which is a Centennial project, will make known an aspect of our history during Confederation. I can think of no better person to record the pages of the past of Government House and its occupants than Dr Hubbard. He has brought to light a story which might otherwise never have been told. I think he has captured the warmth, serenity, and withal the vitality which have characterized Rideau Hall. One feels that happy people have lived here.

CONTENTS

PLATES

NOTE: Sources of illustrations are given in parentheses; illustrations from the Public Archives of Canada are designated P.A.C.

If any justification were necessary for a history of Rideau Hall it would be found in the fact that this house has been the residence of the representative of the Crown, the apex of our constitution, ever since Confederation. And if a reason for its appearance at this moment were to be sought, it would be found in the intensive review of all our institutions which has been undertaken in the years leading up to the centenary of Confederation.

This, however, is not a political history. I must leave to qualified historians a full discussion of political events involving governors-general. Equally I must leave to the political scientists any consideration of the constitutional position of the Governor-General and its evolution over the years. Yet I cannot avoid all reference to these matters, especially when they appear essential to the understanding of this or that figure in history. In such cases, however, my remarks must be limited to facts and to accepted generalities.

One set of generalities to which I can subscribe was written of Lord Lorne some eighty years ago: 'It is no easy thing to be a governor-general of Canada. You must have the patience of a saint, the smile of a cherub, the generosity of an Indian prince, and the back of a camel.'[1] I venture to say that the present distinguished incumbent of the office has these qualifications and many others besides. He and his gracious wife are people whose dedicated lives are an inspiration to us all. We of today must needs regard them not only as heirs to the traditions of the past but the embodiment of the virtues, and the fulfilment of the strivings, of all their predecessors.

I have attempted this study as one who has worked for some years in the field of Canadian art and architecture. But architecture, though important in my account, cannot be the whole story of Rideau Hall. In dealing with the people who have lived there and their contributions to Canadian life I have had to invade the field of the social historian. Whatever may be thought of the results, I have tried to deal in as straightforward way as possible with a rich store of material which is both fascinating and largely untapped, and which I believe is important for all Canadians to know about.

This then is the picture of a house and its life. Geographically, Rideau Hall is but a minute part of Canada, but it has served as a convex mirror to concentrate much of the colour and interest of our history into a small span. In view of the lack of literature on the subject, and owing to the amount of time that is required to carry on research both in this country and in England, I have here been able to cover only the Victorian and Edwardian periods. The rest of the story down to the present day must await a further period of study.

Over the years during which I have been engaged in this work I have accumulated many debts to those who have encouraged and actively helped me. In England, these include the daughters of two governors-general of my period, Lady Evelyn Jones, daughter of Lord Grey, and the late Lady Isobel Gathorne-Hardy, daughter of Lord Stanley. I am grateful also to several members of former households who have established contacts for me: Lord Albemarle, A.D.C. to Lord Grey; Sir Alan Lascelles, secretary to Lord Bessborough and later to King George VI; and Sir Shuldham Redfern, secretary to Lord Tweedsmuir and Lord Athlone. The Librarian of Windsor Castle has kindly supplied photographs from the Royal Archives, and Sir John Summerson has allowed me to consult him as an authority on the architecture of the period of the original Rideau Hall.

In Canada, my source material has come largely from the Public Archives of Canada, where Dr W. Kaye Lamb and his staff have patiently responded to all my requests. I am grateful to Lieutenant-Colonel C. P. Meredith of Ottawa for allowing me to consult his father's invaluable journal. My friend the eminent historian Colonel C. P. Stacey has more than once come to my rescue in the interpretation of the historical backgrounds of my chapters and has prevented me from making many a foolish blunder. And Mr C.C.J. Bond of the National Capital Commission has been generous with his vast fund of information about Ottawa.

Those at the National Gallery who have most assisted me in research and the assembling of illustrations have been members of the library staff: two former members, Mrs Joyce Sowby and Mrs Christa Collin, and the present photograph librarian Mrs Alice Armstrong. Miss Helen Chisholm, Mrs Barbara Boutin, and Mrs Myrtle Clemence have willingly helped in the typing of the manuscript. On the administrative plane, my studies have been made possible by the Board of Trustees, by the former director Dr Charles Comfort, and by the present director Dr Jean Sutherland Boggs.

Special mention must be made of the personal interest taken by the Queen's Printer, M. Roger Duhamel, and his staff in the publication of this book and by M. Henriot Mayer, Superintendent of Translations, and his staff in the preparation of the French version.

At Government House, the constant support of the project from the beginning, and practical assistance given me at every stage, by Mr Esmond Butler, Secretary to the Governor-General, have been absolutely essential to the success of the undertaking.

In the place of highest honour in my procession of benefactors are two governors-general of Canada. The Right Hon. Vincent Massey, C.H., conceived such a history before I ever thought of it and has given me encouragement and advice. But it was Their Excellencies the present Governor-General and Madame Vanier who were the inspirers of my work five years ago. I am particularly grateful to them for their encouragement of it ever since and for their gracious presence at the lectures given at the National Gallery during the winter of 1965-6, which form the basis of these chapters. It is fitting that this book, which has been a labour of love, should be dedicated to them.

R. H. H.

The National Gallery of Canada, Ottawa, September 1966

plate 1

plate 2

CHAPTER ONE / *BEGINNINGS*

As of so much else in and about Ottawa, the origins of Rideau Hall go back to the Rideau Canal[1] (Plate 1). This great and costly work of military engineering was begun in 1826 under Colonel John By of the Royal Engineers. Its purpose was to provide a safe route from Montreal to Lake Ontario, by which the international reaches of the St Lawrence might be avoided in the event of an attack from the south. The locks on the Ottawa River brought into the region gangs of workmen who settled down to populate Bytown. Their chief employer was Thomas MacKay (1792-1855)[2] (Plate 2) a stonemason from Perth in Scotland, who had emigrated to Montreal in 1817 and become a contractor first for the Lachine Canal and later for the Rideau. With his profits of a few years he built several mills at Rideau Falls which had been noted by Champlain and named by early explorers. MacKay may thus be regarded as founder of the village of New Edinburgh which grew up round the mills and later became part of Ottawa. Before his death he had become a railway promoter and a member of the Legislative Council of the Province of Canada.

By 1838 he was rich enough to build himself a stone house[3] measuring 76 by 47 feet on his hundred-acre estate overlooking both the Ottawa and Rideau rivers. With their grudging admiration of success his contemporaries nicknamed the wild land he owned 'MacKay's Bush' and his house 'MacKay's Castle.'[4] The real name of the house was Rideau Hall.

One of the earliest pictures of it occurs as a small detail of a water colour, *New Edinburgh: from the West, or Bytown Side of the Rideau River above the Falls* (Plate 3), which Thomas Burrowes, a member of By's staff, painted in 1845. Castle, or at any rate 'princely mansion,'[5]

9

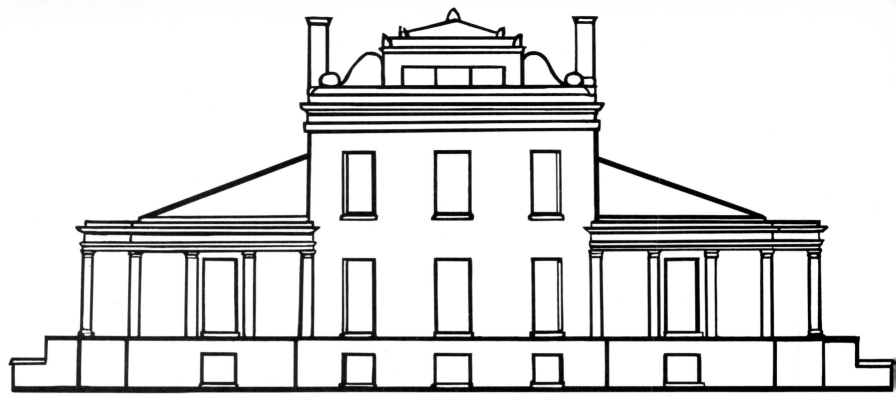

plate 4

plate 3

this house must indeed have seemed in that day of log houses; but architecturally it was something at once more modest and more characteristic of its time, a Regency villa.

In the absence of evidence to the contrary, and in view of the differences the house exhibits, as redrawn to its original form (Plate 4), from the usual late Georgian or Classic Revival product of the period in Canada, we must accept the opinion of MacKay's contemporaries that he designed it 'out of his own head.'[6] But we must still account for its architectural features which, in combination, are unique in Canada. These are a bow-fronted central structure rising through two storeys and an attic, and the two flanking rectangular wings with galleries enclosed by Doric colonnades. The severe lines of the elevation caused someone in the nineteenth century to describe its style as 'Presbyterian' after the strict religious beliefs of the builder. Architecturally, however, it recalls nothing so much as the early villas designed by Sir John Soane,[7] the most individual architect of the Neo-classic in England. Sir John Summerson,[8] curator of Soane's Museum in London, has drawn my

plate 5

plate 6

attention to two villas in particular, Saxlingham Rectory in Norfolk of 1784 and Chilton Lodge in Berkshire (Plate 5) of 1788,[9] as examples of attic storeys on a curve; and to the 'Tivoli' (Plate 6) and Lothbury-and-Bartholomew-Lane corners of the Bank of England of about 1805, as likely sources of the 'monumentalizing' of a curved gable by means of scrolls and acroteria. One can only conclude that MacKay in remote Bytown in 1838 had access to Soane's book *Cottages and Villas* (1793) and to engravings of the Bank of England. It is interesting also to note that in 1818 Soane himself made plans for a Government House to be located at York in Upper Canada (Plate 7), which were never carried out.[10] On a rough sketch for this project, now in Soane's Museum, there is near the right margin a tiny elevation that strongly suggests Rideau Hall.

The original Rideau Hall, dating from the period of the Rebellions and of Lord Durham, is today almost lost to view among the additions made piecemeal over the past century. This may be appreciated in a modern plan of Government House (Plate 8). The west wing of the

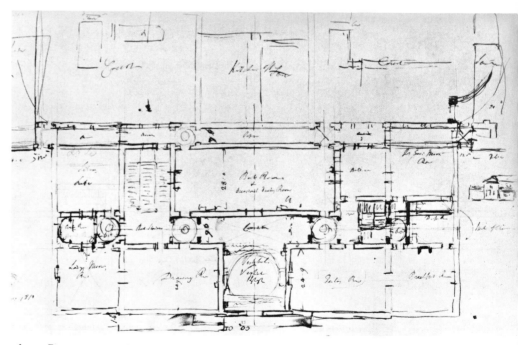

plate 7

11

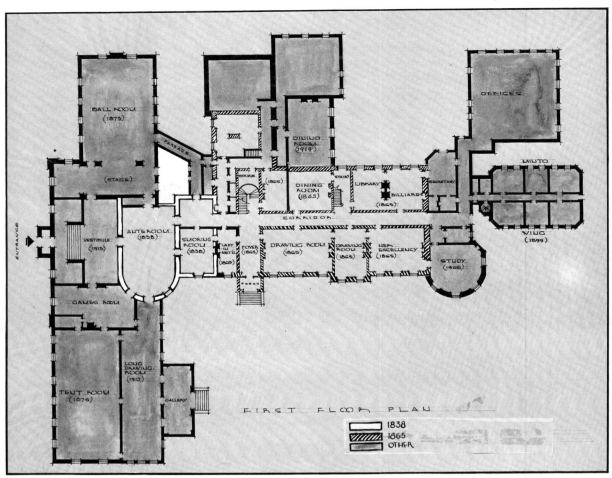

FIRST FLOOR PLAN

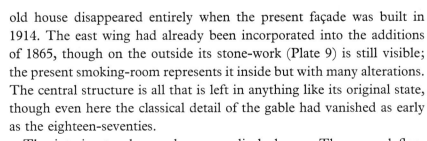

☐ 1838
▨ 1865
▬ OTHER

plate 8

plate 9

old house disappeared entirely when the present façade was built in 1914. The east wing had already been incorporated into the additions of 1865, though on the outside its stone-work (Plate 9) is still visible; the present smoking-room represents it inside but with many alterations. The central structure is all that is left in anything like its original state, though even here the classical detail of the gable had vanished as early as the eighteen-seventies.

The interior too has undergone radical change. The ground floor has lost nearly all its partitions; the long French windows are almost the only remaining original features. The floor plan has been reconstructed by McRae and Adamson[11] (Plate 10); to this I have had to make a few

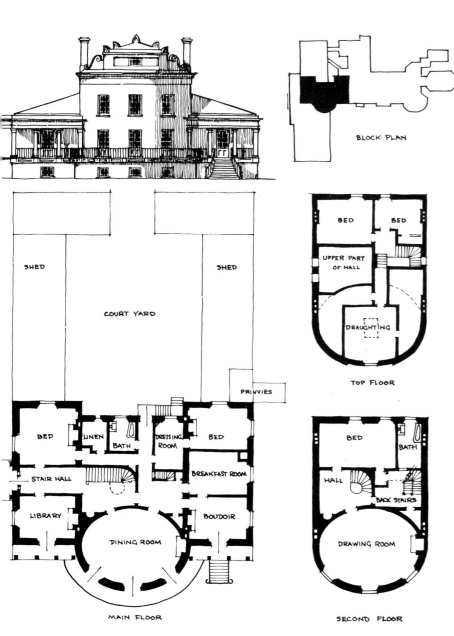

BLOCK PLAN

SHED

COURT YARD

SHED

PRIVVIES

BED | LINEN | BATH | DRESSING ROOM | BED

STAIR HALL

BREAKFAST ROOM

LIBRARY

BOUDOIR

DINING ROOM

MAIN FLOOR

plate 10

BED | BED

UPPER PART OF HALL

DRAUGHTING

TOP FLOOR

BED | BATH

HALL

BACK STAIRS

DRAWING ROOM

SECOND FLOOR

plate 11

corrections on the basis of old documents and plans. The curve of the bow front was occupied on the ground floor by an oval dining-room, connected by a lift to the kitchens below. There were also a 'sitting parlour,' library, nursery, study, one bedroom, and a bath with hot and cold running water—this latter a most unusual feature for the period. From the entrance hall (Plate 11) with its Regency niches a curving stair led to the floor above. Here were two more bedrooms and, 'commanding a magnificent panoramic view of Bytown and the surrounding country,'[12] the main feature of the house, a handsome oval drawing-room (Plate 12). This room, one of the best of its period surviving in Canada, is still intact, having been used (as we shall see) for a variety of purposes

13

plate 12

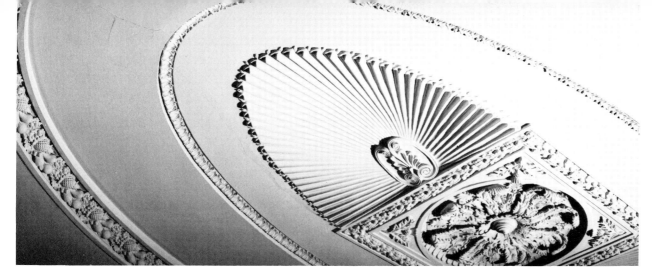

plate 13

plate 14

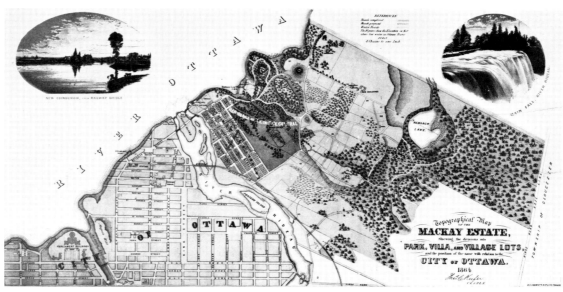

plate 15

before its recent designation as royal bedroom. On its ceiling is a rather splendid array of original plaster mouldings and ornaments (Plate 13), rich in foliage which includes Scottish thistles. There is a marble chimney-piece of chaste classical design. A lesser though still fine stairway, which survives (Plate 14), leads to the attic storey with its three bedrooms and lumber-room. In the basement were kitchen, laundry, larder, wine-cellar, servants' hall and bedrooms, and that ultimate luxury for the period, a hot-air furnace.

Various early visitors to MacKay's 'Elysian retreat' remarked on the 'ornamental wooded grounds' (Plate 15) that surrounded it. A 'serpentine drive and elegant hedges of cedar'[13] led to the main entrance on the west side of the house, and a path led round to the garden door (probably

plate 16

on the east side). On the north, behind the house, was a walled court-yard with an ice-house and carriage house. Beyond lay MacKay's cow barn, piggery, and dairy. There were also, on the south side, flower and kitchen gardens, vineries, and a bowling-green.[14]

As proprietors of the principal mansion of the district, MacKay and his wife Anne Crichton received nearly all the eminent visitors to Bytown. They enjoyed the reputation of being good hosts, Thomas being remembered for his playing on the bagpipes. Their guests over the years included at least two governors, Lord Sydenham in 1840 and Lord Elgin in 1848 and 1853.[15] Doubtless Sir Edmund Head came as well. Water-colour drawings by Lady Head of 'Barrack [Parliament] Hill' are said to have influenced Queen Victoria to choose Ottawa[16]—the name adopted at the town's incorporation in 1855—as capital of the province. On the 2nd of September 1860, the day after he had laid the foundation-stone of the Parliament building (Plate 16), we read that the young Prince of Wales 'took a quiet drive around the city, passing through the beautiful grounds of Rideau Hall.'[17]

By that time MacKay had been dead five years, though the family still owned the house. Ottawa had become the capital, eliciting from

Goldwin Smith the famous description of it as 'a sub-arctic lumber-village converted by royal mandate into a political cock-pit.'[18] But the preparation of the new capital went ahead in spite of political disputes and financial difficulties. In 1859 an architectural competition for the three buildings on Parliament Hill was won by Fuller and Jones (for the Parliament building) and Stent and Laver (for the East and West Blocks). Designs were also sought for a Government House to be built on Nepean Point. Those chosen were a Grecian design by Cumberland and Storm of Toronto (first prize) and a Norman design by Thomas Fuller of Ottawa (second prize).[19] But by 1864, with Parliament nearing completion and the government's move from Quebec becoming imminent, nothing had been done about the governor's residence. As a temporary measure Rideau Hall and some eighty acres were leased from the MacKay estate, through the agency of MacKay's son-in-law Thomas Coltrin Keefer, at a rental of $4,000 a year. Plans were ready by January 1865 for the enlargement of the villa by three of four times its size at an estimated cost of $110,000. Time was to prove this estimate to be barely half the actual cost over the next three years.[20]

The Governor-General of British North America at this point was Charles Stanley Monck, 4th Viscount Monck (1819-1894)[21] (Plate 17), an Irish peer who had been a Lord of Treasury in the Palmerston government. He had arrived in 1861 just at the time of the *Trent* affair to succeed Sir Edmund Head. An able administrator, tenacious and prudent, he was at times a little too discreet and slow to please John A. Macdonald. The great questions of the day were those of defence and the unity of British North America in the face of American expansion and military strength at the time of the Civil War. In spite of the belief that he belonged to the anti-colonial party in England Monck was actually a strong, and in the end a zealous, advocate of Confederation. For this and other reasons he deserves, as Colonel C. P. Stacey has noted,[22] an honourable place among the Fathers of Confederation. In addition, Monck advocated the designation of Canada as a kingdom and of her governor as a viceroy, and the establishment of a Canadian order of knighthood.

In more intimate matters Lord Monck and his family are known to us from the letters[23] he wrote every week to his son Henry at Eton and later at Oxford and from a charming book by a kinswoman, Frances Monck, about her long visit to Canada in 1864-5.[24] These sources

plate 18

reveal the love the country gentleman from County Wicklow had conceived for his Canadian capital Quebec and for his semi-rural seat Spencer Wood (Plate 18), more recently the residence of the Lieutenant-Governor of Quebec and renamed Bois de Coulonge.[25]

On their first visit of inspection to Rideau Hall in 1864, before the additions were even begun, the Moncks were 'much disgusted with the squalid look of Ottawa.'[26] 'We all groaned over Ottawa,' wrote Frances Monck, 'It looks as if it were at "t'other end of nowhere," and we felt so out of the way.'[27] Back in Quebec, she added, 'We had a long horrid moan over Ottawa'[28]—but saved herself in a footnote: 'I little knew how happy I should be there after all.'[29] Monck's family were appalled by the very idea of a move, and irritation grew as the day approached. The matter was not helped by the fact that the previous year, after a fire, he had rebuilt Spencer Wood to his heart's desire. It was well equipped with the racket courts, stables, skating-rinks, toboggan-slides, and conservatories that made his life agreeable; and Quebec was ideally situated for expeditions to the country—little picnics to Montmorency and long fishing trips to Tadoussac. At Spencer Wood he received many a visitor from the least to the grandest, from Tom Thumb to the delegates to

plate 17

plate 18a

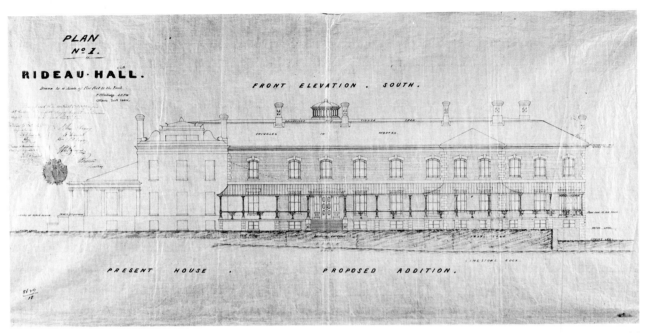

plate 19

the Quebec Conference of 1864.

The government's exodus to Ottawa proceeded apace in 1865 and 1866.[30] Whilst civil servants moved their desks and files, the Department of Public Works began the additions to Rideau Hall. These, like the Parliament buildings, were vociferously opposed by George Brown, the Reform leader. As he complained in a letter to Macdonald, 'The Governor General's residence is a miserable little house, and the grounds those of an ambitious country squire.' Macdonald heartily agreed that 'we have spent more money patching up Rideau Hall (Plate 18a) than a palace would have cost at Nepean Point.'[31] The architect, F. J. Rubidge, reported that the additions were planned 'within as modest a sum as possible and in consideration of the fact that the property was held by the government only for a term of years.' The style adopted was a much simplified version of the current Second Empire, 'it being considered unnecessary that any expense should be incurred to harmonize with the [old].' Another and more curious reason for economy in the design was that Rideau Hall was at a distance from Parliament and thus presumably would not be seen by many of the public.[32] It was

fortunate indeed that the fullest elaboration of Victorian design was avoided; thus at least the additions did not clash with the villa, and in fact the whole building had a dignity and homeliness which all its later occupants came in time to appreciate.

The additions (Plates 19, 20, 21) consisted of a long two-storey wing built on at the east side of the old house.[33] The semi-rough masonry of 'dressed' Gloucester stone made, however, little attempt to match the ashlar of 1838. The upstairs windows with their arched tops were characteristic enough of the Second Empire style, but the simple roof-line lacked the mansards so dear to Victorians. Verandas supported on whimsical ironwork ran the length of the house on the garden side. A belvedere broke the line of the roof, and another such which has since vanished straddled the old house.

Inside on the ground floor (Plate 22) several drawing-rooms of fair proportions on the south side afforded a distant view of Parliament Hill, and a 'family entrance' gave access to the garden. Across a long corridor a smallish dining-room and a bedroom and dressing-room for Lady Monck occupied the north side of the new wing. The upper

18

return as governor-general.[72] This was to be realized more than forty years later when Prince Arthur, Duke of Connaught, arrived at Rideau Hall in 1911.

In 1870 Lisgar received the Grand Duke Alexis of Russia, son of the Tsar, who also made the grand tour of North America. Francis Turville, the Governor-General's secretary—he married Lady Lisgar after her husband's death—quite understandably made both these royal visits occasions for requesting the government to smarten up the house. Such items as bracket lamps, oval tables, and chintz curtains were purchased, and a private boat landing and railway station in New Edinburgh were arranged; but more ambitious projects for windmills and fountains in the grounds had to be set aside.[73]

Lisgar himself made a short tour of the upper Great Lakes in 1870.[74] In October of the following year he paid the first official visit of a governor-general to the United States. On this occasion he met President Ulysses S. Grant at Portland, Maine, for the inauguration of the rail link with Saint John and Fredericton.

On his departure from Canada in June 1872[75] Lisgar was able to say in his farewell speech that he left a Dominion stretching 'from the Atlantic to the Pacific'[76] (Plate 32). For during his period he had seen the great western and northern territories acquired from the Hudson's Bay Company and Manitoba and British Columbia admitted as provinces. But Rideau Hall changed but little. It was left to Lisgar's younger and more colourful successor to extend both the house and the entire scope of the Governor-General's activities.

plate 31a

plate 32

plate 33

CHAPTER TWO / *THE SEVENTIES*

One sunny day in June 1872 a smallish, swarthy man in his mid-forties, strikingly Disraelian in appearance,[1] stood gazing out from the deck of the steamship *Prussian* to catch his first glimpse of Canada. He was Frederick Temple Blackwood, 1st Earl of Dufferin (1826-1902)[2] (Plate 33). By his side, under a parasol, was his young and pretty wife (Plate 34). Their ship had already passed that of the homeward-bound Lord Lisgar whom Dufferin was succeeding as Governor-General of Canada.

Like both his predecessors Dufferin was Irish. He was born in Florence at a time when his father, Price, 4th Baron Dufferin, was estranged from his parents over his marriage and therefore absent from the family seat Clandeboye in County Down. His mother, the Helen of Harold Nicholson's *Helen's Tower*, was one of the three beautiful Sheridan sisters, granddaughters of the dramatist and of Elizabeth Linley; and in the young Dufferin's veins 'the Sheridan blood seethed and tingled like champagne.'[3] In 1856 he made a long yacht voyage to Iceland and Spitsbergen, which he described in *Letters from High Latitudes*.[4] His first public appointment was as a commissioner to Syria in 1860, and in 1864 he became Under-Secretary of State for India and later Under-Secretary for War. In Gladstone's first ministry he was made Chancellor of the Duchy of Lancaster and was advanced to an earldom.

His wife, Hariot Rowan Hamilton,[5] came from another old County Down family, traditional rivals of the Blackwoods. Accompanying them to Canada were their two youngest children, Hermione, three, and Basil, two. The others, Helen, twelve; Archibald Lord Clandeboye, nine; and Terence, six, would join them for the Christmas holidays. Two more were to be born in Canada, making seven in all.

Dufferin's appointment, as Professor F. H. Underhill[6] has noted, gave evidence of a change of attitude towards the Empire on the part of the British government: from the 'Little England' mentality to late Victorian Imperial enthusiasm. Dufferin himself was a very different man from the two staid public servants who had been governors-general since 1867. With his romantic temperament he was just the man to breathe life into his high office and to kindle the imaginations of Canadians with the spirit of Confederation. He was also the right man to set a pattern of life at Rideau Hall which has been followed ever since, and to establish the presence of the Governor-General in all parts of the country. Lady Dufferin was the first wife of a governor-general to play a leading part in Canadian life. Her book, *My Canadian Journal*,[7] mirrors both Canadian society in the seventies and the energy and charm of two characters admirably suited to their roles. I am here following the chronological plan of the *Journal* and allowing its author and her husband (through his many letters and speeches)[8] to speak for themselves as much as possible. In no other period except that of the Aberdeens is there such a wealth of first-hand material to draw upon.

The Canada whose beauties the Dufferins admired[9] as they sailed between the narrowing banks of the St Lawrence was a country, as Lord Lisgar had noted in his parting speech, that now stretched from sea to sea—though Prince Edward Island was yet to enter Confederation. With the worst threats of American domination past, and with plans afoot to connect the provinces by rail, it seemed to many a propitious time. But unfortunately the seventies were also years of economic depression and of political scandal, frustrating the grander dreams of Canadians.

The Canadian people were far from being united. Strung out thinly along thousands of miles, they were divided politically into provinces with separate colonial traditions and culturally into two language groups. In addition to the French who had been settled for two centuries and the Loyalist English who had been here for one, there were multitudes of recent immigrants still to be absorbed. The country badly needed some unifying force. That was what the Dufferins set out to supply. As we so well know today, the task was too great for two people in six years—but that did not daunt them for one moment.

On the 25th of June they disembarked at Quebec, the ancient capital which had seen so many governors come and go. The Prime Minister, Sir John Macdonald, also the possessor of a Disraeli-like face, was on hand to greet them. After a salvo from the Citadel, and the swearing-in at the Parliament building, they left at once for Ottawa.

Here they got the worst over at the beginning. Macdonald wrote to Lisgar that he found Dufferin at first sight 'rather too gushing for my taste.' 'It was amusing,' he continued, 'to see the dismay with which they saw Ottawa and Rideau Hall.'[10] Dufferin himself, in his early letters

home, found Ottawa 'a very desolate place, consisting of a jumble of brand new houses and shops, built or building, and a wilderness of wooden shanties spread along either side of long, broad strips of mud, intersecting each other at right angles, which are to form the future streets of Canada's capital'[11] (Plate 153). But he took an immediate liking

plate 34

to the people: 'Both men and women are dignified, unpretending, and polite, very gay and ready to be amused, simple in their ways of life, and quite free from vulgarity or swagger.'[12] It was for these not untypical Canadians that he and his wife devised a new system[13] whereby every citizen could meet the Queen's representative and virtually everyone who could afford the clothes could attend viceregal functions, a system that avoided the extremes of English rigidity and American laxity and yet preserved an essential dignity. Some at the time inevitably found the Dufferins' entertainments a little too 'mixed,'[14] but Canadian society at its best has retained this equilibrium ever since.

Lord Dufferin described his house as 'nothing but a small villa such as would suit the needs of a country banker.'[15] His wife, unconsciously echoing Lord Monck and his family, wrote in her *Journal*:

We have been so very enthusiastic about everything hitherto that the first sight of Rideau Hall did lower our spirits just a little! The road to it is rough and ugly, the house appears to me to be at the land's end, and there is no view whatever from it, though it is near the river—and we have come through thousands of miles of splendid scenery to get to it! Then I have never lived in a Government House before, and the inevitable bare tables and ornamentless rooms have a depressing effect. . . .[16]

This was written the very day she arrived. 'The morning has brought more cheerful reflections,' she noted the next day. 'We are not intended to live here at midsummer, and I dare say that in winter this place looks lovely.'[17]

By Dominion Day 1872 she had made a start on the house, choosing out the rooms for their various purposes and discovering that 'our vice-regal establishment possesses about six plates and as many cracked tea-cups.'[18] She was also accustoming herself to the aides-de-camp, one of whom was her brother Frederick Rowan Hamilton, who catered to her every wish. Electric bells were being installed and carpets and cretonnes had been ordered from England. Out of doors, a fire-engine had been acquired and a pavilion for the Cricket Club[19] was planned. The Secretary, Colonel Henry Fletcher[20] of the Scots Guards, had his own domestic problem. 'I have brought my wife [Lady Harriet Fletcher] & children (five in number) to Canada,' he wrote to the minister of Public Works, '& the house built for the Governor General's secretary is too small to contain us.'[21] During the summer plans were prepared by the chief architect of Public Works, Thomas Seaton Scott, for an upper storey to be added to Rideau Cottage[22] (Plate 35).

Meanwhile the Dufferins had left for Tadoussac on the lower St Lawrence, where they fished and chose the site for a house.[23] At the same time workmen at the Citadel in Quebec were 'whitewashing the barracks' in which (as Dufferin wrote to the Colonial Secretary in London) 'we shall have to rub on for this year.'[24] In reality the house, a former officers' quarters, was quite a good example of Regency military architecture (Plate 36). When he moved into it Dufferin discovered the view from the Citadel to be 'as splendid a landscape as I have seen in any part of the world.'[25] A few alterations and some new wall-paper had made an old mess room downstairs into a good dining-room, and the

plate 35

drawing-room upstairs opened on to the superb platform above the river.[26] The Dufferins were the first to use the Citadel as a viceregal residence in the old capital, Spencer Wood having become the residence of the Lieutenant-Governor of Quebec; and it has been cherished by their successors ever since. In August and September, during the election campaign and Macdonald's victory at the polls, they held a ceaseless round of entertainments: three or four dinners a week, luncheons, teas, and even breakfasts; levees, balls, sports meetings, and band concerts. They made frequent expeditions to the country and availed themselves of the Governor's traditional privilege of access to the old Quebec convents, the Ursulines, the Hôtel-Dieu, and the Hôpital-Général.

Early in September the Dufferins received the English astronomers who formed the British section of a joint survey party to establish the 49th Parallel of latitude as boundary in the west between the United States and Canada. The leader, Captain Samuel Anderson, R.E., in a letter home, described Lord Dufferin as 'most agreeable and affable.'[27] Lady Dufferin, he noted, 'looks about twenty, is very pretty, and is full of conversation.'[28] The surveyors were to revisit the Dufferins the following year when their mission was accomplished.

Later that month the household embarked on their first official trip, Lady Dufferin being the first wife to accompany a governor-general on

plate 36

plate 37

31

plate 38

tour. The itinerary on this occasion was limited to southern Ontario[29]—Toronto, where they visited every institution in the city and admired the Norman building of the University, Hamilton, Niagara, and London—but the happy balance they struck between friendliness and dignity set a precedent for all later tours. At its conclusion they settled in Ottawa for the autumn and winter. From the beginning their life in the capital included frequent short trips to Toronto and Montreal. On one such occasion Dufferin unveiled the statue of Queen Victoria in Montreal, speaking in both French and English, and on another they received a boisterous welcome from the students of McGill University (Plate 37).

Lady Dufferin now took a fresh look at her house:

Rideau . . . is a long, two-storied villa, with a small garden on one side of it and a hedge which bounds our property on the other—so that at this time of year there is really no place to walk. . . .

The gentlemen try to ride every day, and come back covered with mud. I walked into the town one day with Dufferin, and the following paragraph appeared in the evening paper:

"Lady Dufferin.—It would astonish some of our fine ladies to see Lady Dufferin walking about the town. She dresses plainly and sensibly, wears thick boots, and does not shrink from the muddiest of crossings."

This comes of my Irish training![30]

That autumn the house was full of workmen making alterations and installing gas chandeliers. The decorators were there too. The Governor-General's study received red-covered furniture and green curtains and was hung with his own sketches and portraits. A skeleton which he used for anatomical drawing dangled in a corner to terrify visitors. Lady Dufferin's 'boudoir' was pink and had views of Ireland on its walls.[31] But she still complained of the principal rooms and their 'hopelessly company look;'[32] in order to relieve this she bought much new furniture from Arnoldi in Montreal.[33] In the grounds, Rideau Cottage was nearly finished, and a a telegraph wire was run up to the Hall.[34] The children played at football, stilts, and hoops while they waited for the skating-rink to be made ready.

An ordinary day[35] at Rideau Hall began with breakfast at nine. Then the A.D.C. went out to inspect the horses and returned to write invitations. At eleven the Governor-General and suite went to the office in town, which had been opened in the East Block on Parliament Hill.[36] There he dealt with despatches, received members of Parliament, and presided over formal meetings of the Privy Council. After lunch at home and various afternoon outings came tea, children's games, reading, and dinner at half-past seven. By then, however, the day had hardly begun.

In the evenings, after the opening of Parliament, the Dufferins held a series of balls in the oval room upstairs[37] (used for this purpose for the present and later as a morning-room), musical parties in the drawing-room, and dinners—which Meredith the diarist found too heavy for his taste[38]—for all officials and members of Parliament in their turn. To these, during the Christmas holidays, were added children's teas and skating parties. Lady Dufferin describes one of the latter:

Skating is so very graceful when well done, and the scene on the rink is so gay; every one moving about so fast on the ice, and knots of people tobogganing down the hill behind. I had on my skates, but did not feel equal to skating before such experts.

When it became cold, we came into the house, drank tea and mulled claret, and danced for an hour. We intend to repeat these parties once a week.[39]

On New Year's Day 1873 there was a levee at which Lady Dufferin helped her husband receive the 293 men who came to pay their respects. Because of all this activity Dufferin began to complain to the Colonial

plate 39

Secretary about his salary. He could do 'very little either for Art or Literature' at his present rate.[40] 'I cannot,' he had written earlier, 'keep my house in Ottawa from freezing under an annual expenditure of £1200 or £1300.'[41] He was in fact using his own funds prodigally, believing that there was 'a considerable sphere in which one could employ ones self to advantage by promoting the amalgamation of the French and English races, and the social fusion of the various provinces.'[42]

After attending the winter festivities in Quebec and Montreal he opened the new curling-rink (Plates 38, 39) he had built at his own expense at Government House.[43] It never lacked for use. Nor did the large new ballroom[44] (Plate 40) which the government added at the north side of the main door. Before its actual completion it was inaugurated on the 13th of March, a week after the opening of Parliament, with all of its 94 gas burners[45] round the walls blazing with light. Lady

plate 40

plate 41

plate 42

Dufferin was delighted with it:

The guests assembled at nine, and after having some tea were conducted through unknown passages (Plate 41) to their future ball-room, where they found 300 chairs arranged in rows, in front of a very pretty little stage, and a band dressed in the gorgeous uniform of the Governor General's Guards. The entertainment began with music, and was followed by "To Oblige Benson," which went off admirably. People were particularly delighted with Fred's performance. . . .[46] (Plates 42, 43).

There was more music and then supper for all three hundred. Plays[47] appear to have been the favourite amusements during Lent when balls could not be held. Far from being great literature for the stage, they nevertheless afforded the spectators the greatest enjoyment.

The first ball in the new room was held after Easter. Twists of muslin and bunches of pink roses were hung round windows and doors to disguise the lack of paint in the unfinished room, and a throne covered with crimson velvet was placed at the far end opposite the stage.[48] The six hundred and fifty people present that evening gave indication that the enlargement of the house would allow much greater scope to vice-regal entertaining.

In the spring, with Lady Dufferin taking time out to hear the debates

plate 43

on the Pacific Scandal, over the building of the Canadian Pacific Railway, in the House of Commons, there began a series of outdoor receptions culminating in a big garden-party in May with a tent, a band, and dancing afterwards. It is astonishing to hear, in the midst of it all, that a daughter, Victoria, was born on the 17th of May.

Three weeks later the family left for Quebec. Reaching Tadoussac in June, they found the new house ready (Plate 44). 'It is so pretty,' wrote Lady Dufferin, 'with red roof, green blinds, and white walls. We have a platform, upon which we sit and look out upon the St. Lawrence, and on to which all the sitting-rooms open.'[49] It still stands, as does the Fletchers' cottage near it.

In July, after fishing (Plate 45) on the Mingan River and in the Gaspé, they began a tour of the Maritime Provinces. On arrival at Charlottetown on the 18th, a few weeks after Prince Edward Island became part of Canada, Dufferin could report that 'Nothing could have been more joyous and exuberant then our reception.' He opened a railway, watched a regatta, and attended a picnic 'at which a great deal of champagne was drunk, and a judge nearly killed by a runaway horse he undertook to groom.'[50]

By this time the Pacific Scandal, which so compromised his Prime Minister, had flared up furiously. For this and for purely Nova Scotian reasons Dufferin was nervous when they reached Halifax. His reception on landing from the yacht *Druid* was cool,[51] but the temperature rose perceptibly during his stay. Then, leaving his wife behind, he hurried back to Ottawa to prorogue Parliament, rejoining her at Saint John, New Brunswick. Feeling himself 'in a devil of a mess,'[52] he nevertheless received a cordial welcome that included a torchlight procession. By his energy and personal charm he did much to hold the country together in the crisis.

After his return to Ottawa in October politics took a fateful turn. Parliament met and the embattled Prime Minister made his famous five-hour defence in the House of Commons, with Lady Dufferin present to hear it. Then followed Macdonald's resignation and the formation of a new government under the Liberal leader Sir Alexander Mackenzie. Perhaps it was some consolation to the Dufferins in the midst of the turmoil that Rideau Hall had been much improved during the summer by such additions as crimson carpets in the passages and white paint round doors and windows.[53] The Secretary's room had been enlarged and refurnished with a blue-covered table and a wash-hand-stand.[54]

The new season closely resembled the last but was even more packed with activity. The Governor-General being ill on New Year's Day 1874, his wife received the gentlemen by herself.[55] That winter, besides the very numerous dinners, plays, and balls, we hear of a magic lantern showing, of 'tableaux' posed by the beauties of Ottawa, a concert in aid

plate 44

of St Bartholomew's Church, an ice ball in Montreal, a twenty-one mile sleigh ride in the Gatineau, and curling matches in the new rink, at which the dour new Prime Minister 'brightened up very much during the "roarin' game".'[56] Lady Dufferin gives the first account of an indoor amusement which everyone who lived in the house during the next forty years was to recall so vividly:

. . . we tried to light the gas, and I had the satisfaction of succeeding three times, myself. I held a piece of wire, or a needle, in my hand, rubbed my feet on the carpet, and touched the burner; a spark was emitted, and the gas instantly blazed up.[57]

A few visitors arrived. One was the clergyman-novelist Charles Kingsley[58] who in this last year of his life came to preach in Ottawa. Another was Laurence Oliphant,[59] the English journalist and traveller, who had been Lord Elgin's secretary in Canada. Dufferin had met him in the street and invited him to Rideau Hall to explain the strange religious community in the United States to which he belonged.

In the spring of 1874, after Mackenzie had won the election and Parliament had opened, the Household went up the Gatineau River to watch the logging; attended the review of troops on the Queen's Birthday, at which Lady Dufferin presented colours to the Governor-General's Foot Guards,[60] and then the proroguing of Parliament; shot the timber slide at the Chaudière Falls; and picnicked at Meach Lake.

After the customary summer fishing—Lady Dufferin caught the largest salmon that year—they set out on another tour. It began in Toronto and proceeded to Lake Simcoe (where Dufferin gratuitously counselled the Ojibway Indians to avoid firewater),[61] then Muskoka, Georgian Bay, and Lake Superior (where he painted some Indian portraits), and on to Thunder Bay. On the return journey they called at Chicago where they inspected the damage caused by the great fire of 1871, and Lady Dufferin admired the new Palmer House hotel with its furniture in the Egyptian style.[62] Then came a visit to Detroit and their re-entry into Canada at Windsor, where the Governor-General addressed the citizens in French. After this followed a whole series of Ontario towns including Sarnia, Berlin (now Kitchener), Guelph with its model farm, Brantford and the old Mohawk chapel, London, Woodstock, and Ingersoll—where the main feature of their reception was an immense cheese which when cut was found to contain bottles of champagne.[63] Next came Niagara Falls where they inspected the new International (Suspension) Bridge built by their friend Colonel Casimir Gzowski, the Polish émigré engineer; and finally Toronto, where there was a regatta. Lastly they visited the Lake Ontario towns. Each one had built an elaborate welcome arch for them to pass under. In his speech at Brockville Dufferin gave a résumé of them all: arches composed of cheeses, salt, wheels, hardware, stoves, pots and pans, sofas, chairs, ladders with firemen, carriages, boats, children, and even lovely young ladies.[64]

In September and October they paid their first official visit to the United States.[65] In New York they saw a number of plays and met Bret Harte, the author of stories of mining-camp life, and Albert Bierstadt, the painter of western landscapes.[66] With the latter they struck up a warm friendship, inviting him to Canada a number of times and thus bringing his influence to bear on the Canadian artists who later painted

plate 45

the Canadian west. Dufferin went alone to Washington for a meeting with President Grant, after which he and his wife visited Boston and met all the literary lights: Longfellow, Emerson, Richard Henry Dana, and Oliver Wendell Holmes.[67]

They were back in Ottawa for the winter sports. The children had already made a huge snow-man which blocked the view of the town by day and was illuminated by night.[68] But best of all was the new toboggan-slide (Plates 46, 47) described by Lady Dufferin:

The new slide is most exciting, for, the natural hill not being considered sufficiently steep, a great addition has been made to it. A long flight of stairs now leads to the top of a high wooden slide, and, as this is almost perpendicular, the toboggan starts at a rapid rate down it—and its occupant has both the length and the excitement of his slide greatly increased. To-day the wooden part of the slide is a sheet of ice, so the toboggans rush down it at a tremendous pace.[69]

plate 46

In November the 49th Parallel survey party visited Ottawa on their way home. Captain Albany Featherstonhaugh, R.E., performed in one of the theatricals, *Wooing a Wife*. Captain Anderson in a letter home wrote that Lady Dufferin drove about in an open sleigh completely enveloped in a 'cloud,' 'a long woollen comforter, which goes round and round the neck and round the head and then a yard or two to spare.' A third member, Lieutenant William Galwey, returned black and blue from the slide to write to his mother, 'It is a most favourite amusement at Government House. Ladies go in for it. I think they like rolling over and over with the gentlemen.'[70]

At Christmas there was a fairy-tale play and a tree for the children, with the gas-lights going out just at the moment for the presents. On New Year's Day 1875 the usual reception was held, both wine and tea being served. In the midst of the winter revels a son Frederick was born— but he did not delay proceedings for long. By March Lady Dufferin was rehearsing an operetta, *The Maire de St Brieux* (Plate 48) with lyrics by the children's tutor Frederick Dixon and music by Frederick Mills, the Cathedral organist.[71] 'I asked the actors to keep on their costumes during the evening,' she wrote, 'and they made the party look very gay and pretty, the girls' colored petticoats and high, white caps, and the men's bright-colored clothes being very effective.'[72]

After a period of home leave in England, from May to October, the Dufferins returned to Canada accompanied by their new secretary, Colonel Edward Littleton[73] of the Grenadier Guards, who replaced Fletcher. Another vigorous season began. In November Dufferin in-augurated the Supreme Court of Canada in their 'red robes and ermine.'[74] In January 1876 a children's play was marred but not halted by a gas fire near the stage; it is remarkable that dangerous mishaps such as this never stopped anyone or anything for very long. Albert Bierstadt was staying in March and painting a picture for Lady Dufferin.[75] Presumably it was of Government House, and perhaps it will be recovered one day (Plate 49).[76]

By March a large wooden structure,[77] variously called tennis court, tent room, and supper room (Plates 50, 51, 52), had been hastily built at the south side of the main door, balancing the ballroom on the north. Lady Dufferin thought it very pretty, 'with its red-and-white tent, let

plate 47

plate 48

plate 49

plate 50

40

plate 51

plate 52

down inside the tennis court, and shields bearing the arms of the various provinces hung round the walls.'[78] On the 22nd of March a Grand Fancy Dress Ball was held for 1,500 guests, the largest crowd yet accommodated (Plate 53). The Dufferins, dressed as King James of Scotland and his queen, presided over elaborate singing quadrilles, waltzes, and lancers and a hearty repast in the tent room lasting until four in the morning.[79]

The house at this point acquired some new furnishings, the list of which forms an interesting catalogue of Victoriana, including as it did such items as silver baskets for the dinner table in the form of fisher-boys, sedge-warblers' nests, and kneeling cupids on shells. Also purchased were 33 dinner plates, 14 baths, two foot-baths, two croquet sets, and one rat-trap.[80] In the grounds a large circular gasometer[81] (Plate 54), which still stands, was built to manufacture gas from crude petroleum and presumably to avoid the uncertainties of the city mains.

In the summer, after Quebec and the Gaspé, the household and accompanying newspaper reporters embarked on their longest trip of all, from Ottawa to the west coast.[82] They took in their railway carriage such assorted supplies as plates, knives and forks, tea, jam, preserved meats, eggs, and Devonshire cream.[83] As the Canadian Pacific Railway was still a decade short of realization, they went by way of Chicago and the Palmer House ('oh, so smart!'[84]) and on to Omaha. Here they boarded one of Pullman's Palace Cars for Cheyenne and thence across the Rocky Mountains to Odgen and San Francisco. Here, after being met by General Sherman, they were shown the new cable cars, and they set out for Vancouver Island in H.M.S. *Amethyst*.

At Government House, Victoria (Plate 100), Dufferin received deputations of British Columbians who threatened secession from Confederation because of the delays in building the Canadian Pacific. After visiting Port Simpson, Alert Bay, and other Indian villages, and New Westminster and the Fraser River he returned to Victoria to deliver his famous and very long Columbian Speech.[85] Prefacing it with grandiloquent paragraphs on the rosy future of this 'glorious province,' he went on to explain the government's position in the matter of the railway. This public assumption of effective authority was the prelude to his clash with his ministers. Meanwhile, returning by way of San Francisco, the Dufferins were enchanted with the Chinese theatre in that city and broke the long journey home with halts at Salt Lake City (to observe the Mormons), Denver, St Louis, and Toronto.

Immediately on arrival in Ottawa Dufferin left for Philadelphia to see the Centennial Exposition. The Canadian section[86] met with his hearty approval. In the exhibition as a whole he saw evidence of 'the great Anglo-Saxon race indestructibly united,'[87] thus anticipating the Imperial mystique of 1900.

By November his personal efforts to solve the Pacific problems through the intervention of the Colonial Office had involved him in a serious dispute with the Cabinet. We have his own word for it that in a terrible interview with Mackenzie and Edward Blake on the 18th of the month they nearly came to blows.[88] The once exuberant Governor-General who at the outset had proclaimed himself 'as the Chief of the Executive of Canada, as the representative of the British Crown, and as the servant and spokesman of the British people'[89] had now to acknowledge the realities of responsible government. In his frustration and isolation at Rideau Hall he wrote to the Colonial Secretary, 'I am getting quite sick of this business.'[90] Earlier he had written, 'One's life at times is dull and lonely. Luckily I have been able to take to the Winter amusements of the Country and with skating and curling get plenty of exercise.'[91] And again, 'I shall be glad when my term is over.'[92] He also read Greek[93] and practised his drawing[94] to fill in the rest of the time.

There was, however, no let-up in the social life. Quite the contrary in 1877. In January the Dufferins paid an extended visit to Toronto. In a speech to the Toronto Club the Governor-General commended the efforts of the Ontario Society of Artists and called on the government to establish a national gallery,[95] an institution which was to come into being in Lord Lorne's day. In a more important address, at the National Club, he referred to the change in his status. His much reduced duties, he said, were

. . . very similar to those of a humble functionary we see superintending the working of some complicated mass of steam-driven machinery. (Laughter.) This personage merely walks about with a little tin vessel of oil in his hand (renewed laughter), and he pours in a drop here and a drop there, as occasion

plate 53

plate 54

plate 55

or the creaking of a joint may require, while his utmost vigilance is directed to no higher aim than the preservation of his wheels and cogs from the intrusion of dust, grits—(roars of laughter again and again renewed)—or other foreign bodies.

Continuing in more serious vein, he described the Governor-General in very significant terms, as

A representative of all that is august, stable, and sedate in the country; incapable of partisanship, and lifted far above the atmosphere of faction, without adherents to reward or opponents to oust from office; docile to the suggestions of his Ministers, and yet securing to the people the certainty of being able to get rid of an Administration or Parliament the moment either had forfeited their confidence. (Applause).[96]

This speech, when reported in England, drew praise from Tennyson and brought a lump to the throat of the Duke of Argyll.[97]

The remainder of that season was marked by one or two unusual if minor events. In April the cabmen of Ottawa presented Dufferin with a gold-headed stick and an illuminated address[98]—and with good reason, as they had enjoyed a roaring trade on account of the many entertainments at Rideau Hall. In June one of the rare diplomatic dinners was given for the Papal Delegate, Bishop Conroy.[98a] At that time Canada had no foreign representatives except for the Delegate and a few consuls in the principal cities.

In the summer of 1877 the Dufferins again spent June at Tadoussac. In August they undertook another western tour, this time to Manitoba. Again their route lay through Chicago. Then, at St Paul, their railway carriage was nearly overturned in a scuffle of striking railwaymen.[99] From there they continued by Red River boat to Winnipeg. Using Donald Smith's model farm Silver Heights on the Assiniboine as his headquarters, Dufferin held many receptions and made many speeches including one in French at St Boniface; sketched the buffalo on the prairie; and powwowed at length with the Indians. Lady Dufferin inspected the transcontinental locomotive[100] (Plate 55) which is named for her and now stands outside the Winnipeg station. They also made camping trips to Lake of the Woods and Rat Portage (now Kenora) (Plate 56) and along the Assiniboine River, visiting Icelandic and Mennonite settlements along the way.

By this time Dufferin's activities had justified his long-awaited increase in salary. What had cost him so much in his first few years, he wrote, was 'getting the steam up' in Canada.[101] Past were the disappointments of 1876, and his term of office had been extended by some months.[102]

The steam was well up in 1878, the last year of his stay. January brought the usual round of winter festivities, with young Clandeboye home from Eton for the holidays. There were many, many parties at Rideau Hall and several visits out of town. In Montreal, in February, Dufferin received great ovations from every quarter including the Art Association, where he announced Bierstadt's gift of a large canvas, *In the Sacramento Valley*.[103] In Toronto, addressing the School of Art, he predicted the founding of a Royal Academy;[104] this became a reality a few years later.

Back in Ottawa the Dufferins held a great farewell party, their last in the new ballroom. The plays on this occasion were two farces, *Sweethearts* by W. S. Gilbert and *New Men and Old Acres* by Tom Taylor, with Lady Dufferin in the leading roles.[105] At the end of the evening the Governor-General read an epilogue in verse, ending in lines that brought tears to the eyes of many:

> And oft, at home, when Christmas fire-logs burn,
> Our pensive thoughts instinctively will turn
> To this fair city with her crown of towers,
> And all the joys and friends that once were ours.[106]

By now they were preparing their departure. 'The house is full of packing-cases,' wrote Lady Dufferin, 'and everything bare and miserable-looking, and I am glad of a rest and holiday.'[107]

Meanwhile the government had paid its farewell tributes in the Senate chamber.[108] In reply Dufferin waxed warm with emotion: 'I found you a loyal people, and I leave you the truest-hearted subjects in Her Majesty's Dominions . . . men of various nationalities—of English, French, Irish, Scotch, and German descent, working out the problems of Constitutional Government with admirable success.' Lady Dufferin found it a very melancholy occasion.[109]

Her last big affair was a bazaar in May in aid of the parish church.[110] There were Punch and Judy Shows, bands, fish-ponds, raffles, and a picture-gallery,[111] all of which went on for three days and brought in enough money to make a gift to the Orphan Asylum over and above paying the debt on the church. Also in May there was a demonstration of that modern marvel of science, the phonograph:

Two men [was Thomas Edison one of them?] brought this wonderful invention

plate 56

for us to see. It is quite a small thing, a cylinder which you turn with a handle, and which you place on a common table.

We were so amazed when we first heard this bit of iron speak that it was hard to believe that there was no trick! But we all tried it. Fred sang "Old Obadiah," Dufferin made it talk Greek, the Colonel sang a French song, and all our vocal efforts were repeated.[112]

On the eve of their departure from Ottawa the City Council held a farewell reception in the new city hall in Elgin Street.[113] In his speech on this occasion Dufferin graciously recalled that two of his children had been born in the capital whose 'regal outline' he had come to love. The family had never 'passed six happier years than we have done beneath the roof of Rideau.' (Plate 57). He and his wife were much affected by this ceremony.[114]

Then dawned the last morning. 'We had to get up early and be at the boat by seven,' wrote Lady Dufferin:

It was trying: first we had to say good-by to all the people about our house.... The large guard of honor was drawn up on the top of the cliff, and at the water's edge were the friends.

A number of young men—the bachelors—were waiting for me on board with a bouquet and silver holder; then the ship began slowly to move away, and there were long cheers and waving of handkerchiefs till we were out of sight. Ottawa looked lovely as we left, and never shall we forget our happy six years here and our innumerable friends.[115]

Her sentiments were to be echoed many times by her departing successors over the years.

The Dufferins left a different Ottawa from that which had greeted them in 1872. It was considerably livelier and had some awareness of its destiny. Thanks to their ceaseless efforts Canada as a whole now had some sense of unity. The role of the Governor-General had become at once better defined and more arduous, and his wife's position greatly enhanced. The stage was set for the arrival of royalty in the next régime.

Meanwhile, during the summer, the Dufferins enacted a long epilogue to their reign. They had some fishing on the St Lawrence, paid a final visit to Boston for Dufferin to receive one of Harvard's rare honorary degrees, bade farewell to their beloved Citadel, and made a tour of the Eastern Townships of Quebec. All this took place during the election campaign in the autumn of 1878, and one of the Governor-General's last acts was to swear in Macdonald and his Cabinet. Then he laid the foundation-stone of Dufferin Terrace, which was shortly to fulfil his wife's description of it as 'one of the loveliest walks in the world.'[116] In one of his (very) last speeches he could announce to Canadians with

plate 57

plate 58

plate 59

some justification that he had become one of them 'in thought and feeling.'[117] He left Quebec on the 19th of October, his wife having taken an earlier ship.

His years in Canada were followed by greater glories for him. With his combination of imperialism and cosmopolitanism he steadily rose to the top of his profession through ambassadorships in St Petersburg and Constantinople and the viceroyalty of India, to end his career as ambassador successively in Rome and Paris. His services were recognized by his advancement as Marquess of Dufferin and Ava in 1888, and he retired to Clandeboye in 1895—only to meet with financial ruin shortly afterwards.[118] Through the years Lady Dufferin retained her energy and sprightliness. He died in 1902 and she in 1936 (Plates 58, 59).

plate 60

plate 61

CHAPTER THREE / *THE EIGHTIES*

The announcement in 1878 that royalty would occupy Rideau Hall caused a stir that affected nearly everyone in the land from the least to the greatest. Shopkeepers hurriedly ordered souvenir articles such as pressed-glass cream jugs and sugar bowls stamped with the heads of the Marquess of Lorne and Princess Louise[1] (Plate 60). The Prime Minister took time out from the election campaign to busy himself with etiquette, a new carriage for the Princess, and a special corps of guards to protect her.[2] And the prospect of a royal court in Ottawa sent shivers of excitement up and down the spines of Canadian Society.[3]

In November Sir John Macdonald, exhausted after his victory at the polls, journeyed down to Halifax. Arriving somewhat the worse for wear, he nevertheless managed to appear, 'pale but erect,'[4] in time to see the Duke of Edinburgh's barge take Lorne and Princess Louise ashore from the steamship *Sarmatian* under an escort of galleys from the Royal Navy. It was at two in the afternoon of the 25th when the young couple— he was thirty-three and she thirty—set foot on Canadian soil. Then

followed the swearing-in, a great reception, and a torchlight procession.[5] At Montreal, *en route* to Ottawa, they attended the St Andrew's Day Ball and saw the city illuminated at night.[6]

Two of Lorne's predecessors, Monck and Dufferin, had urged the elevation of Canada into a viceroyalty[7] but had seen their suggestions turned down for fear of offending the United States. When however, Disraeli arranged for a royal lady to come to Ottawa, it was, as Professor W. S. MacNutt has observed, part of a new 'experiment in statecraft by which the Crown was employed as an instrument to proclaim the greatness and unity of the Empire.'[8]

John Douglas Sutherland Campbell, Marquess of Lorne (1845-1914)[9] (Plate 61) was the eldest son of the 8th Duke of Argyll, chief of the Clan Campbell. He was born at Stafford House, the London residence of his maternal grandfather the Duke of Sutherland. As a child he was strikingly handsome, as Queen Victoria noted in her journal on a visit to Inveraray in 1847:

Outside stood the Marquis of Lorn [*sic.*], just two years old, a dear, white, fat, fair little fellow with reddish hair, but very delicate features, like both his father and mother: he is such a merry, independent little child. He had a black velvet dress and jacket, with a "sporran," scarf, and Highland bonnet.[10]

He was idolized by his family, among them his sister Frances, who has described him as a young man: .

... he had an uncommonly fair complexion, with straight regular features, and the brightest of blue eyes, the whole crowned, as it was to the end of his days, by a wealth of yellow gold hair. A cricket ball slightly destroyed the perfect outline of his nose....[11]

After Cambridge he sat in the House of Commons as Liberal member for Argyllshire, spending part of his time as secretary to his father at the India Office. He was often at Buckingham Palace where his ideal Victorian blend of nobility and dreaminess[12] further endeared him to the Queen. An amateur of poetry, he is well known to Canadians for one of the psalms he rendered into verse, 'Unto the hills around do I lift up.'[13] He was also the friend of painters like Landseer and Millais. In 1866 he visited North America, stopping at Washington and Boston (where he met Longfellow) and just missing a Fenian raid at Fort Erie. He noted his impressions of several Canadian towns at the time: Toronto was dull, Kingston pretty, and Ottawa (where he stayed with the Moncks) impressive with its Gothic towers.[14]

Princess Louise (1848-1939)[14a] (Plate 62) was the first member of the Royal Family in many years to marry a commoner. As painter, sculptor, and writer she fully shared her husband's interests. At their wedding in St George's Chapel, Windsor, in 1871, her curly brown hair, blue eyes, regular features, and 'elegant figure' were much remarked on.[15] The Duke of Argyll, however, noted that she could 'look very grave, almost severe.'[16]

Disraeli broached the matter of the governor-generalship in July 1878 and reported to Lorne on his audience with the Queen:

The Queen, when I first spoke of it, thought that she would not like her daughter to be so far, but on considering that Canada is now only ten days off, and that you might come home for a time every year, and after sleeping over it, she was quite in favour of the proposal.[17]

Queen Victoria herself noted the same occasion in one of her letters:

... I was rather divided in my feelings; satisfaction at the distinction for Lorne, and the fine, independent position for dear Louise; but uncertainty as to her liking to leave her home interests, and go so far away from all her family. The thought, too, of parting from her for so long was very painful. Still, I would not object or oppose the offer, but asked Lord Beaconsfield to make it himself.[18]

Lorne found Canada in better condition than had Dufferin. The Great Depression was ending, and the worst dangers of external en-

plate 62

croachment and (for the time being) of internal disturbance, were past. National pride had begun to swell once more, and spirits were high on his arrival in Ottawa.

The welcome he and Princess Louise received in the capital[19] dispelled the gloom of a rainy December afternoon. 'Captain Stewart's new and handsome troop of Dragoon Guards' formed a cavalry escort,[20] and the Civil Service expressed its feelings in a welcome arch that outshone all previous examples of this florid Victorian genre (Plate 63). Another arch covered the entrance to Rideau Hall (Plate 64).

The house itself (Plates 65, 74) had undergone considerable improvement in preparation for them. The tent room, hastily run up in 1876, was given a permanent foundation and was faced with brick to harmonize it with the ballroom.[21] A telephone was installed.[22] A log skating hut, a new laundry house,[23] and additional staff houses were built in the grounds. At the Citadel in Quebec a ballroom was being added.[24]

Lorne set down his first impressions of Rideau Hall in a letter to his father:

Here we are settling down in this big and comfortable House, which I tell

plate 63

plate 64

plate 65

plate 66

plate 67

Louise is much superior to Kensington, for the walls are thick, the rooms are lathed and plastered (which they are not at Kensington) and there is an abundant supply of heat and light. Snow has only begun to fall and there is not half an inch of it on the ground. . . . The view of Ottawa, with its nests of houses crowned by the Towers of Parliament is really fine, and altogether Rideau is a much pleasanter place than my recollection of it allowed me to think it would be.[25]

The faint note of persuasion sounded here suggests that Princess Louise was not quite as enthusiastic as he.

She however, by now had 'everyone working arms off'[26] making alterations to the inside of the house. Out of doors the 'Princess Vista' (Plate 66) was being cut through the woods to afford a view of the Ottawa River.[27] When these things were done it was time for the usual round of skating parties (Plates 67, 68) to begin.[28] They were not nearly so 'royal' as had been expected.[29]

Lorne kept up the office which Dufferin had opened in the East Block on Parliament Hill but would not use the 'throne' in which he was told his predecessor had presided over the Privy Council during deliberations.[30] He resolved to observe the normal royal practice of acting only on advice. A test arose in the Letellier affair. Hesitating at first to accept his Prime Minister's advice in the serious matter of dismissing a lieutenant-governor on political grounds, he in the end acceded and avoided a conflict with the ministry.[31]

His secretary, the 'excellent' Francis de Winton,[32] now occupied Rideau Cottage (Plate 69). Also living in the grounds were the comptroller, Richard Moreton, and his Greek wife. Their eight-year-old daughter Evelyn (as she was in 1878) many years later, as Lady Byng, recalled how the children of the household went to Rideau Hall for daily lessons and how, enveloped in buffalo robes, they revelled in sleigh rides and the toboggan-slide (Plate 70). In their sealskin coats and great mufflers they went for Sunday walks, with Lorne and Princess Louise heading the sedate procession.[33]

At Christmas three hundred Sunday-School children came for tea and presents. One little boy then, who grew up to be Lieutenant-Colonel C. P. Meredith, still remembers pounding the table for plain bread and butter instead of the fancy cakes he was given. Another young guest at the party asked the Princess how her mother was and received the royal reply, 'Her *Majesty* is very well, thank you.'[34] And on New Year's

plate 68

plate 69

Day 1879, with Queen Victoria at Osborne complaining in a letter of her 'poor Loosy far away in a distant land,'[35] the Governor-General received the gentlemen in the Parliament building and not at home as formerly.

The engagement diaries for these years fortunately survive to record the roster of events.[36] Dinners were given for as many as fifty members of Parliament a week; Parliament was opened in 'royal weather';[37] and viceregal visits were paid to the House of Commons to hear Macdonald at the top of his form. Princess Louise's artist friends, Henrietta and Clara Montalba[38] of London, were staying, the former modelling a bust of Lorne in fur collar and cap[39] (Plate 150), the latter being painted by Louise[40] (Plate 71). Both works still exist. The men of the Household went out shooting moose and bear along the Ottawa.[41] And of course there were theatricals in the ballroom[42] (Plates 72, 73).

At about this time material was being gathered for an article on Rideau Hall that appeared in *Harper's New Monthly Magazine*. Its author was Annie Howells Fréchette,[43] wife of the Canadian poet Louis Fréchette and sister of the American novelist William Dean Howells. Though catering to her American readers' fascination with royalty, Mrs Fréchette informed them that life here was so unaffected as to approach 'almost a republican simplicity.'[44]

A 'royal standard'[45] flew over the house (Plate 74). Below, from the skating hut, the Princess could survey the winter amusements:

The toboggan slide and vicinity fairly blossoms with the merry, romping company. Surplus dignity is thrown to the winds, along with streamers of ribbons, tassels, and bright-hued scarfs. A pretty Canadian girl never looks prettier than when clad in her cloak made of a fleecy white blanket . . . a red or blue *tuque* perched coquettishly upon her abundant hair . . . and a bright colored skirt just showing between her cloak and moccasined feet. Put a toboggan and two or three beaux at her disposal, and she is happy (Plate 75).[46]

On the evening of a ball the guests were received in the ballroom, which had soft green walls and gold and white ornament, red curtains, and a large tapestry at the far end. At midnight a Scottish piper led the way to supper in the tent room.

The Princess, 'like so many English women,' rode and walked a great deal and was always '*sensibly* shod and dressed.'[47] Some of the curious complained of never seeing her face for her veil, but that was because

plate 72

plate 73

plate 74

plate 75

plate 76

she suffered from neuralgia. She sketched constantly, using a portable hut (Plate 76) which could be moved about the grounds, regularly inspected the kitchens, and took a keen interest in the parish church, to which she gave a peal of bells.

The rooms[48] had an 'air of culture and refinement.'[49] Adjoining the conservatory was Princess Louise's 'blue parlour' (Plates 77, 78) with its blue paper and curtains, old tapestries from Scotland, and chairs with antimacassars embroidered with pink and blue daisies. On the chimney-piece stood an ebony and blue porcelain clock; and there were gilded cages of canaries. Though it was in this room that she decorated the doors with sprigs of apple blossom, the only painted door surviving, is now in the corridor[50] (Plate 79). Next came the green and

plate 77

white library, with its new tiled chimney-piece[51] on which stood a bronze clock crowned with a bust of Queen Victoria. French and German books lay open on the tables. The drawing-room (Plate 80), with grey paper and red carpet, contained a piano, a display of Sèvres porcelain, and 'countless and costly knick-knacks.'[52] There was also a studio (Plates 81, 82) for painting and music; it was probably upstairs next to Thomas MacKay's oval drawing room, which was now being used as the Governor-General's bedroom.

Cricket and lacrosse, an English and a Canadian game respectively, were played in the grounds that spring. The gardens were being improved (Plate 83). A trip was made down the Ottawa on a log 'crib' with an exciting climax at the timber slide near the Chaudière Falls.

plate 78

plate 79

plate 80

plate 81

plate 83

plate 82

plate 84

59

plate 85

plate 86

The usual review of troops on the Queen's Birthday became a special event with the Princess in attendance. And there were visits to Montreal, on one of which Lorne opened the Art Association building in Phillips Square, paying tribute in his speech to Canada's photographers and great operatic soprano Emma Albani, and envisaging an Academy of Arts to encourage the growth of a Canadian school of landscape painting.[53] He was in fact already conferring with the Toronto artist Lucius Richard O'Brien on the subject of an academy.[54]

In June they stayed at the Citadel in Quebec for the first time (Plate 84). On the 9th Lorne opened Dufferin Terrace[55] (Plate 85), that inspired achievement of town-planning begun under his predecessor. The next day his father, a brother, and two sisters arrived from Scotland. On the 11th Princess Louise laid the foundation-stone of the new Kent Gate, Queen Victoria's gift to Quebec; and on the same evening they attended a *Cantata of Welcome* composed by Calixa Lavallée.[56] It is small wonder that the Duke of Argyll exclaimed at the 'party spirit' that prevailed in Quebec. He also noted his son's intense interest in everything Canadian, including the plants, birds, and fishes.[57]

The entire family then sailed down the St Lawrence to fish and paint in the Gaspé[58] (Plates 86, 87). In August Lorne and Louise made their first tours of the Maritime Provinces and Ontario. On the latter trip stops were made at Toronto (where Lorne opened the Exhibition, chose new furniture at Hay's shop,[59] and bought a horse), Hamilton (where he admired the view of the bay from Dundurn), Brantford, London, Guelph, and Berlin (where he made a speech in German).

When back in Ottawa the Princess was reported by an English newspaper to have suffered an attack of melancholy.[60] There was also a dark rumour, much fostered by the political opponents of the Prime Minister, that Macdonald had offended her by appearing drunk at a ball.[61] For his part, however, the Prime Minister could only express jubilation over a Governor-General who had supported his appointment of a high commissioner to London. 'Lord Lorne,' he wrote, 'is a right good fellow, and a good Canadian.'[62] Princess Louise, however, departed for England to stay about four months.[63]

One day in January 1880 a reporter and an artist arrived from New York. The article they published in *Frank Leslie's Illustrated Newspaper* opens on a solemn note:

The door was opened by a stalwart sergeant . . . who was attired in England's

plate 87

plate 88

61

plate 89

plate 90

plate 91

plate 92

red. Another orderly-sergeant stood at attention, while a sentry gazed grimly at me as, Martini-Henry on shoulder, he paced backwards and forwards. . . .[64]

Whereupon the reporter entered the outer hall, with its chocolate-brown paper, and then the inner hall decorated with the Montalba bust of Lorne, Chelsea china, majolica, and statuettes. After calling at the secretary's 'snug and cheery' office (Plate 88)—probably the present smoking-room—and negotiating the long red-carpeted corridor he at length arrived at His Excellency's study (second from the end on the left) (Plate 89).

The Marquis of Lorne was seated at a cabinet-desk close to the window, a buffalo robe enshrouding his chair. He was attired in a blue shirt with a turned-down collar; a brown scarf, a blue coat with Astrachan collar and cuffs, and braided in black silk after the fashion of a hussar-jacket. His trousers were of light plaid, his boots laced, with yellow tops and india-rubber soles. He wore no ornaments save a massive gold watch-chain of the curb pattern, and two plain, lumpy gold rings.

"Welcome to Canada!", he cheerily exclaimed, as, starting from his chair, he advanced to meet me with extended hand.[65]

The study, which looked out over the rinks, had grey walls, green carpet, a marble chimney-piece with a mirror, and a tapestry. On the scarlet-covered desk stood a wonderful inkstand made of a hoof of Lord Clyde's charger in the Crimea.

Lorne slipped into a blanket coat and they went outside. Here follows a flamboyant description of tobogganing and the 'champagney feeling' one got going down the slide (Plate 90). Then there was lunch in the dining-room (Plate 91) with its dull red walls hung with Dutch landscapes and royal portraits by Winterhalter. Walnut sideboards supported gold salvers, claret jugs made of horn, and a silver biscuit box in the shape of a drum. Several stuffed ducks completed the Victorian *décor*. 'It was late in the evening,' the writers concludes, 'when I took my leave of the blue-blooded Laird of Lorne.'[65a]

Princess Louise returned in February (Plate 92), and W. J. Topley took his photographs of the household on the rink[66] (Plate 93) which were to be reproduced a good many times over. Then came the opening of Parliament and the state dinner. All this was but prelude to the accident on St Valentine's Day, which is reported in the engagement diary:

14 February. The Day fixed for the 1st Drawing Room. At 8:15 p.m. His Excy., HRH & Suite left Government House in 3 sleighs. The Covered Sleigh in

which were His Excy., HRH, Mrs Langham & Col. McNeil [MacNeill], was overturned close to the gates, the horses having bolted. The sleigh was dragged on its side for 400 yards, & was stopped by Mr Bagot [A.D.C.][66a] & a groom. . . . The Drawing Room postponed sine die.[67]

Lorne himself filled out the story in one of his letters:

L. has been much hurt, and it is a wonder that her skull was not fractured. The muscles of the neck, shoulder, and back are much strained, and the lobe of one ear was cut in two. As we pounded along, I expected the sides of the carriage to give way every moment, when we should probably have been all killed. As it was, L. was the only one much hurt.[68]

Queen Victoria's displeasure has only to be imagined; but Lorne flatly stated that his wife was henceforth forbidden to winter in Canada.[69] Some Ottawans were disgruntled at the sudden cessation of public entertaining and therefore of trade.[70] We hear too of mutterings among the ladies of Ottawa that the Princess had found them somewhat less amusing than the vivacious and educated ladies of Quebec.[71] The retreat of a sensitive woman from life in the isolated capital is understandable

enough, but what few at the time knew was that regular warnings were being received of Fenian attempts on her life.[72] Fortunately, the records afford a few glimpses of her true character. On one occasion during an epidemic of scarlet fever she herself cared for the sick at Rideau Hall when the maids refused to do so.[73]

Yet in spite of all there was considerable activity that winter and spring. Arthur Sullivan took time out from the American tour of *The Pirates of Penzance* to visit Rideau Hall.[74] While in Ottawa he set to music the words of Lorne's 'A National Hymn' (Plate 94):

God bless our wide Dominion,
    Our fathers' chosen land;
And bind in lasting union
    Each ocean's distant strand;
From where Atlantic terrors
    Our hardy seamen train,
To where the salt sea mirrors
    The vast Pacific chain:
O bless our wide Dominion,
    True Freedom's fairest scene;
Defend our people's union;
    God save our Empire's Queen.[75]

Though neither the words not the rumbustious tune, first played by the Foot Guards band, ever caught on, they gave added proof of Lorne's enthusiastic Canadianism.

By this time not only was he advocating a permanent defence force, for Canada[76] but he and Princess Louise were hatching the Canadian Academy of Arts.[77] With L. R. O'Brien,[78] its president-elect, they chose the pictures for the first exhibition and nominated the charter academicians. Macdonald arranged the purchase of the Clarendon Hotel in Sussex Street,[79] where, on the 4th of March 1880, in the presence of all the leading lights of Ottawa, he inaugurated the Academy[80] (Plates 95, 96) and with it the National Gallery which was implied in its charter. With the newspapers[81] reporting more promenading than looking at pictures and a hopeless mix-up of hats and galoshes, one gathers that openings of exhibitions then were not very vastly different from those of today. In view of the fact that Lorne's critics had called the Academy premature by at least a century,[82] it was no mean achievement in an age of materialiam. Only a governor-general could have carried it off.

On Good Friday Princess Louise attended church for the first time since the accident, and Lorne went off to hear the new organ at Christ Church. Late in May they went to Quebec to meet the *Sardinian* with

DOMINION HYMN.

plate 94

plate 95

Queen Victoria's youngest son Prince Leopold aboard. A grand review of troops was held on the Plains of Abraham before he and his sister departed for Chicago, the Mecca of all visitors to the New World. Lorne stayed behind, visiting his new summer house on Lake St Charles.[83] The royal party, on their return, sailed down to the Cascapedia River for the fishing, Lorne again remaining in Quebec for the Saint-Jean-Baptiste Day celebrations, at which Lavallée's 'O Canada' was first sung.[84] It was to have a considerably longer life than Lorne's hymn.

At the end of July Princess Louise sailed back to England with her brother on a visit that was to last eighteen months. In her absence one or two newspapers insinuated that she disliked Canada;[85] and one who styled himself 'Captain Mac' printed a scurrilous pamphlet entitled *Canada: from the Lakes to the Gulf*,[86] which hinted at all sorts of mischief concerning the Lornes and included a coarse satire on an investiture at Rideau Hall. A Mr and Mrs J. Muggins Jones, a retired eating-house keeper and his wife, are haughtily met by 'the first high keeper of the door bell.' In the presence of royalty Jones is made to sprawl on the

65

plate 98

plate 97

plate 96

66

floor by 'the usher of the red bamboo' before receiving the knighthood for which he has paid in hard cash[87] (Plate 97).

To return from this nonsense to the autumn of 1880, Lorne undertook his second tours of the Maritime Provinces and Ontario, complaining all the while that he was the victim of the 'annual autumn epidemic of "Fairs".'[88] But lest the impression be gained that his life was purely social, it should be noted that at this time he was taking an active part in the final Canadian Pacific Railway contract.[89]

In November he attended an improbable-sounding football match between Ottawa and Harvard University, saw Buffalo Bill perform, and heard the Jubilee Singers, the famous Negro Spirituals group. Then, in the early part of 1881, there followed more skating carnivals and plays. In May, at the Citadel, he was visited by his uncle the Duke of Sutherland and the Rev. Dr James ('Hamish') McGregor of Edinburgh.[90] When this Presbyterian divine was taken to visit one of the old convents of Quebec he without warning began to question the nuns about their underclothing, 'wishing apparently,' Lorne wrote, 'to get at a hair shirt, but getting only a general giggle from the whole line.'[91] After an investiture in the Citadel Lorne was moved to urge a Canadian order of knighthood on the Colonial Office;[92] but this like Monck's proposal before it came to naught. He then unveiled the statue of de Salaberry at Chambly, by Philippe Hébert.

In July it was 'Westward Ho! for the great plains and rivers, and the wild Indians.'[93] In order to focus British attention upon Canada he deliberately chose the difficult Canadian route for this his first western tour. Stopping first at Toronto, he inspected the wood-engravings being made for Principal G.M. Grant's ambitious publication *Picturesque Canada*.[94] Then the party, which included Dr McGregor and several correspondents for British newspapers,[95] sailed from Owen Sound to Port Arthur and thence proceeded overland to Winnipeg. At Portage-la-Prairie, the end of steel, they began the really strenuous part of the journey. Riding by day and camping out by night, they passed through the Qu'Appelle Valley and on to the Saskatchewan River, where they took a steamer to Prince Albert. On the 9th of September they first sighted the Rocky Mountains, and after a great Blackfoot powwow lasting until three in the morning[96] (Plate 98) they followed the Bow River to Calgary. Leaving Canada to take the easier route home, they stopped at Helena and Boulder before boarding the train for Council Bluffs, St Paul, and Winnipeg.

The exhausted Lorne departed in November for home leave in England. He returned in January 1882 with his sister Frances, who has left interesting accounts of the winter sports in Ottawa, but who decided that the 'Land of Ice and Snow' was not for her.[97] The frontier seemed indeed close that year. In March Lorne was visited by a Blackfoot chief, and in May he went bear-shooting in the Rockcliffe woods just behind the house.

The main event of the spring was the birth of his 'other Canadian child,'[98] the Royal Society of Canada. Ever since he had encountered a Smithsonian expedition from Washington in the Canadian west he had been devising a scientific and literary institute for Canada.[99] After a preliminary meeting in 1881, and some little bickering on the part of the scholars, he inaugurated the Society in the Senate chamber on the 25th of May.[100] A day or two later, accompanied by his learned guests Dawson of McGill, Chauveau, Faucher, Le Moine, and Lawson, he visited his first child, the National Gallery, on the first day of its opening in the Old Supreme Court building.[101]

In June Princess Louise appeared in Canada for the first time since 1880. The Colonial Secretary had written to Macdonald of the Queen's serious concern for her daughter's safety,[102] and extra guards had been posted at Rideau Hall.[103] For the time being, however, she and Lorne rested in the safety of the Citadel, where she painted[104] (Plate 99) and rode her pony, and at Tadoussac where they both delighted in watching the whales and seals.[105]

Macdonald was uneasy over the long trip through the United States which they commenced early in September.[106] But Lorne, like Dufferin before him, was anxious to conciliate British Columbia over the continuing delays in railway construction. With the Canadian Pacific still far from finished, the tour began as usual at Chicago, where General

plate 99

plate 101

perament, however, was different from that of his enthusiastic predecessors, as appears in one of his many letters to his mother: 'I like to dwell on the sunny side of our life here, but don't imagine that sea sickness is the only sickness which the passage of the Atlantic brings to one who loves his home as passionately as I do.'[129]

The Citadel and the summer fishing came as pleasant reliefs from 'the lumber yard of Ottawa.'[130] One visitor to their house in the Gaspé[131] was Lady Lansdowne's brother Lord Frederic Hamilton.[132] This lively chronicler of his times accompanied them to Quebec. The 'home-like feeling'[133] he noted at the Citadel was no doubt produced by the many furnishings they had brought with them from Bowood, the Lansdowne seat in Wiltshire.

Lord Frederic duly arrived at Rideau Hall, where he jumped at the sparks that leapt from the footman's silver tray and from the brass fender in his bedroom in winter, and played the time-honoured game of lighting the gas jet by static electricity.[134] Of the town he wrote, perhaps a little rosily:

The Ottawa of the "eighties" was an attractive little place, and Ottawa Society was very pleasant. There was then a note of unaffected simplicity about everything that was most engaging, and the people were perfectly natural and free from pretence.[135]

The winter sports fascinated him. At one curling match between Ottawa and Montreal the ice was coloured and the long-distance telephone was first used to communicate the score to Montreal.[136] The Lansdownes and their two daughters—one was to become Duchess of Devonshire and to return to Rideau Hall in 1916—were expert skaters, and all Ottawa turned up to their 'Arctic Cremornes' for which an ice-house was built with thin sheets for windows.[137] Always in the background, 'Seen from Rideau Hall in dark silhouette against the sunset sky, the bold outlines of the conical roof of the library and the three tall towers flanking it gave a sort of picturesque Nuremberg effect to a distant view of Ottawa'[138] (Plate 110). After the skating, supper was served in the rink by footmen wearing fur coats.[139] Skiing was introduced in January 1887.[140]

Very little was done to the house. But a set of account books survives to give some idea of the dinners that were served to satisfy the mighty appetites of the eighties. In April and May 1888 Lapointe's fish and game shop in the market-place filled orders for clams, smelts, brook

trout, muskellunge, partridge, woodcock, plover, quail, and once as a special treat the horrifying total of twenty dozen snow-birds. Bate, the grocer in Sparks Street, supplied ginger-ale, potted hare, truffles, toothpicks, and fly-paper as well as the more ordinary items.[141]

In the summer of 1884 Lansdowne opened a meeting of the British Association for the Advancement of Science, on the first occasion on which that body met in Canada. But above all in importance that year

plate 109

was the Rebellion brewing up in the west. The clash came in March 1885, with Lansdowne rather underestimating the 'disagreeable little outbreak'[142] and Quebec's reaction to it, but considering it important enough to allow Melgund to join General Middleton as chief of staff.

In October 1885, after the Rebellion but before the last spike of the Canadian Pacific was driven, the Governor-General rode across the prairie to smoke the pipe of peace with the Indians and arrived at Calgary to attend what sounds like an early Stampede. But the flatness of the country appalled him. 'Nothing,' he wrote, 'would induce me to live there.'[143] Continuing westward, he eventually reached the haven of Victoria: 'If I had to live on this continent I should pitch my tent here.'[144]

plate 110

74

plate 111

plate 112

On his return to Ottawa he found the Fisheries Dispute with the United States coming to a new head. In 1886 in the midst of the negotiations, while he was on home leave, he entreated the Colonial Office not to leave Canada in the lurch again.[145] In May 1887, after Macdonald's victory in the elections, he had a crisis of his own to deal with. An Irish Radical who had arrived to stir up sympathy in Toronto gave cause for alarm when the Governor-General arrived to celebrate Queen Victoria's Jubilee. But with the Queen's Own Rifles on hand in civilian clothes,[146] Lansdowne met only with a 'triumphant reception' and fervent expressions of loyalty.[147] Toronto could still be counted on.[148]

In the same year Joseph Chamberlain, a future Colonial Secretary and like Lansdowne a breakaway Liberal, visited Rideau Hall and was photographed in the conservatory (Plate 111). The Governor-General, noting the excellent impression his visitor had made as head of the British delegation to Washington,[149] reported on him more personally to his mother:

Chamberlain has made himself very agreeable to us all. . . . He is a pleasant member of society; light in hand, a good talker, and as far as one can judge frank and outspoken.[150]

Chamberlain the imperialist was to make his mark on Canada in the appointment of Lord Minto as Governor-General in 1898.

Lansdowne, one of Canada's ablest governors-general since Confederation, departed a little prematurely, having been appointed Viceroy of India. In his farewells he could report on the 'peaceful progress of industry, education, and art' during his stay. Warning against Reciprocity with the United States, he called for the improvement of imperial defence; but he had become enough of a Canadian to prefer spontaneous action by the Dominion to more formal arrangements.[151] His later life in India and at the War Office is too well known for recital here. He died in 1927.

His successor, it must be acknowledged at the outset, is best known to Canadians today as the donor of a famous trophy for hockey (Plate 112). Sir Frederick Arthur Stanley, 1st Baron Stanley of Preston (1841-1908)[152] (Plate 113), was a son of the Earl of Derby, the British prime minister. He became a Conservative member of Parliament, held Cabinet posts, and was raised to the peerage in his own right in 1886.

Accompanying the Stanleys to Canada in 1888 were four of their ten

plate 113

plate 114

children. I had the good fortune to meet the second youngest, Isobel,[153] in London not long before her death in 1964 at eighty-nine. She vividly recalled the five years of her girlhood spent in Ottawa and showed me her mother's albums from those years. These began with newspaper cuttings of their arrival in Montreal. The new Governor-General is described as in the prime of life, with a ruddy complexion, full beard, blue eyes, a 'strong frame,' and something of the bearing of the Prince of Wales. His wife Constance[154] had brown hair and 'large and pleasant features;' she wore a striped summer costume and carried a parasol. With them were the Military Secretary, Captain Josceline Bagot,[155] who was to live at Rideau Cottage, and three aides-de-camp who included two of the Stanleys' sons (Plate 114).

On her arrival in Ottawa Lady Stanley did not dare to remove the 'hideous blues and reds'[156] left over from Princess Louise's decorations. In this connection it is interesting to learn that Queen Victoria once rebuked Lady Stanley for calling the house Rideau Hall: it must be Government House as in all other colonial capitals.[157] Lady Stanley, whom Sir Wilfrid Laurier described as 'an able and witty woman,'[158]

plate 115

plate 116

left as her legacy to Ottawa the Lady Stanley Institute in Rideau Street, which she founded for the training of nurses[159] (Plate 115).

The Stanley albums contain records of many parties and balls and of concerts[160] and theatricals[161] (Plate 116) in which the parts were taken by members of the household. It is said that the Stanleys, like the Lisgars, liked to have lights out by midnight; but we hear also of 'free and easy' sleigh rides, skating parties, a fancy-dress carnival with Lady Isobel appearing as Cinderella, and a cake-walk at Mid-Lent.

Sport (Plates 117, 118) figured more prominently than ever before. Hockey was being played by 1892, when we hear that the ladies were becoming enthusiastic about the matches. The Governor-General was a keen fisherman, and in the albums there are pictures of Stanley House,[162] the rambling frame house he built on the Bay of Chaleurs, and which now belongs to the Canada Council (Plate 119). There are also photographs of the western tour of 1889 (cf. Plate 120) and of the railway car *Victoria* which had been built for the purpose. It contained lobby, drawing-room, dining-room, bedroom, bath, and kitchen and had plate glass windows and electric-blue plush seats with lace edges.

There are pictures too of the Citadel in the summers. For one splendid party the rooms were hung with bunting and cooled with blocks of ice; on the platform, decked with green boughs and Chinese lanterns, were little tents for spooning (Plate 121). A grand ball was held in 1890 for the second visit to Canada of Prince George (Plate 122), now twenty-five and in command of a gunboat.[163] In his honour there were waltzes, schottisches, polkas, lancers, and a *quadrille d'honneur*.

Lady Isobel Gathorne-Hardy also produced for me a parcel of letters which turned out to be her father's day-to-day correspondence with Sir John Macdonald.[164] The letters touch on many political topics including the Fisheries Dispute but are most remarkable for their reflection of the real affection which Stanley had for a Prime Minister who by May 1891 was very seriously ailing:

Our official & other relations have ripened into something far more than ordinary friendship.
     To stand by & see you overtaxing your strength, without saying a word, is impossible.[165]

Macdonald died on the 6th of June. Stanley attended the lying-in-state, then called on Sir John Abbott to form a government. Abbott

plate 117

plate 118

plate 119

plate 120

plate 121

soon resigned and in 1892 was succeeded by Sir John Thompson.

Shortly after succeeding his brother as Earl of Derby in 1893 the Governor-General departed from Quebec to the singing of 'Auld Lang Syne.'[166] In later life he held no important office but devoted himself mainly to philanthropy.

Among his visitors in Canada had been Lord and Lady Aberdeen,[167] who spent the autumn of 1890 in Canada. When in 1893 it was announced that Aberdeen would be the next Governor-General, Lady Aberdeen sought Lady Derby's advice on the house. The latter replied:

You will find the furniture in the rooms very old-fashioned & not very pretty; but it is a most comfortable house, & we have become very fond of it; the red drawing room . . . had no furniture except chairs & tables, we brought out a book case & two smaller bookcases which are writing tables as well—they are Chippendale & belong to me. If you care to buy them, I ask £100 for the three. . . . The walls are absolutely bare—we brought out a large collection of old prints we happened to have. . . .[168] The room which has always been the wife of the G.G.'s sitting room is very empty. . . .

. . . There are no lamps in the house at all. No cushions, no table cloths, in fact none of the small things that make a room pretty & comfortable.[169]

Such is the story of Rideau Hall: the handing on of a barely furnished house from one family to another, the character of the house consequently changing with the people. Yet, as we have seen, something was always left behind in house or grounds to mark each occupancy. More importantly, each family left in perpetuity to Canada some legacy, achievement, tradition, or germinal idea.

plate 122

plate 123

CHAPTER FOUR / *THE NINETIES*

When Lord Aberdeen was appointed Governor-General in 1893, he and his wife (Plate 123) were no strangers to Canada. They and their children had crossed the Atlantic in the late summer of 1890,[1] having as their fellow-passengers several prominent Canadians, Sandford Fleming the engineer, Dr William Osler, and Sir John Thompson, then Macdonald's Minister of Justice. After stops in Quebec and Montreal they settled in Hamilton where they had been told the weather was good all year round. At Highfield (Plate 124), a rambling Gothic Revival house at the foot of the Mountain, they spent several happy months. 'The whole atmosphere,' wrote Lady Aberdeen, 'was permeated with sunshine, and crowds of lovely butterflies'[2] (Plate 125). After this they visited Ottawa where they met the Stanleys, Sir John Macdonald, and Sir Donald Smith. Then followed a trip to the west. Their stay in Winnipeg saw the founding of the 'Lady Aberdeen Association for Distribution of Literature to Settlers in the West,' an organization which foreshadowed her later activities in Canada. After inspecting some Scottish crofter settlements in Manitoba they bought a property in the Okanagan Valley in British Columbia, named Guisachan[3] after Lady Aberdeen's father's estate in Scotland. Lady Aberdeen described the whole trip in a small book, *Through Canada with a Kodak*,[4] illustrated with her own snapshots.

She was the dominant partner of the two. A significant proportion of the Aberdeen papers in the Public Archives of Canada emanate from her. Her *Canadian Journal*, a selection of which was published in 1960, has been described as the best social portrait of Canada of its time.[5]

Ishbel Maria Marjoribanks (1857-1939)[6] was the daughter of Dudley Coutts Marjoribanks (afterwards Lord Tweedmouth), a member of Parliament and close friend of Gladstone. Her early life was divided between London and Guisachan, the deer forest in Inverness-shire which her father was reclaiming as farm land. Tall and handsome in appearance, with vivid dark eyes and wavy brown hair, she had a personality to match: warm, generous, and brave. She blossomed out as

plate 124

plate 125

the 'Bonnie Fechter' of her daughter Marjorie's book, after her marriage in 1877.

John Campbell Gordon, 7th Earl of Aberdeen (1847-1934),[7] was the grandson of the Prime Minister of the fifties and succeeded to the earldom in 1870. Slight of build, with smooth dark hair and beard, and of a gentle and sympathetic nature, he was nevertheless a keen sportsman. With his religious and moralistic turn of mind, he naturally gravitated towards the 'high idealism' of Gladstone.

A decisive influence on them both was Henry Drummond (1851-1897),[8] the Scottish theologian and scientist and author of a famous book, *Natural Law in the Spiritual World*, in which he attempted to reconcile Christianity and evolution. His liberal, humanistic, and evangelical teachings did much to soften the effects of the Aberdeens' traditional upbringing. Under his inspiration Lady Aberdeen threw herself wholeheartedly into social services, beginning on their own estates in Aberdeenshire. There she established cottage hospitals, district nursing, Saturday-night classes for workers, Sunday-Schools, staff magazines,

and the Haddo House Club for their immediate household staff. This 'socialistic' treatment of servants scandalized a good many people at the time.[9]

In 1886 Gladstone appointed Aberdeen Lord Lieutenant of Ireland. Devoting themselves to social work and to folk-arts and industries, the Aberdeens won such a measure of popularity as no occupant of Dublin Castle had enjoyed for many years. But after only six months the defeat of the Home Rule Bill, and of the Gladstone government itself, brought their stay to an end.

They then took a trip around the world, on which they were thronged by *émigré* Irish folk wherever they went. In the United States, where they visited Lord Tweedmouth's ranch in Texas, they made a start on their wide circle of American friends. These were eventually to include Andrew Carnegie, Mrs Potter Palmer, and the Vanderbilts among the very rich, Oliver Wendell Holmes and President Eliot among the literary figures, and Phillips Brooks, Dwight L. Moody, and Frances Willard among the religious and humanitarian leaders.[10]

Back in England during the social unrest of the late eighties, they worked tirelessly at charitable causes of all sorts. Lady Aberdeen's health broke down under the strain and they made their escape to Canada in 1890. She of course recovered to plunge even more deeply into her work. In 1891 she prepared the Irish exhibit for the World's Columbian Exposition in Chicago, a village complete with cottages, dairy, and colleens selling lace. On the same trip they met Theodore Roosevelt, Wilfrid Laurier, and the pioneer American social worker Jane Addams. Extending their trip to the Okanagan Valley, they bought another and larger farm, Coldstream Ranch[11] (Plate 126), and planned to grow fruit on a large scale.

On Gladstone's return to power in 1892 the Aberdeens expected to return to Dublin, but the Prime Minister offered them a choice of other posts. They chose Canada. Before taking up the appointment, however, they made a special journey to Chicago to open the Irish Village. On the eve of their final departure for Canada, John Hay, a future American ambassador to London, wrote in their visitors' book an impromptu verse:

> Ask me not here to turn a careless rhyme—
> It ill would suit the solemn place and hour,
> When Haddo's Lord bears to a distant clime
> The Gordon conscience backed by Britain's power.[12]

At the time of their arrival in Quebec on the 17th of September 1893 Aberdeen was forty-six and his wife thirty-six. They were accompanied by rather a large household[13] (Plate 127). Two of their four children, Marjorie, twelve, and Archie,[14] eight, were with them; the two elder boys Lord Haddo, fourteen, and Dudley, ten, were in school but would come out for the holidays. There were also the Secretary, Arthur Gordon, a cousin of Aberdeen's; four aides-de-camp including Captain David Erskine the comptroller; a private chaplain, a personal physician, a shorthand writer, Lady Aberdeen's private secretary, and a Swedish governess, Ebba Wetterman, who has been credited with introducing skiing into Canada[15] (but see page 73).

At Quebec to meet them were the Prime Minister, Sir John Thompson, and several of his Cabinet, and their friend Henry Drummond who that year was giving the Lowell lectures in Massachusetts. On their first evening in the Citadel, Drummond held a private service at which, taking his text from Psalm 46, he spoke movingly of cities and rivers and of the good that should flow from the Aberdeens into Canada.[16]

plate 126

At the swearing-in ceremony Aberdeen expounded in English and French his conception of his office:

If, and because your Governor-General is in the service of the Crown, he is, therefore . . . in the service of Canada.

In other words, aloof though he be from actual executive responsibility, his attitude must be that of ceaseless and watchful readiness to take part . . . in the fostering of every influence that will sweeten and elevate public life; to . . . join in making known the resources and developments of the country; to vindicate, if required, the rights of the people and the ordinances and Constitution, and lastly, to promote by all means in his power, without reference to class or creed, every movement and every institution calculated to forward the social, moral, and religious welfare of the inhabitants of the Dominion.[17]

In their first few days in Quebec Lady Aberdeen engaged a French tutor for the whole family and a dancing master to teach them Canadian steps. She enthused in her journal over the superb view from the Citadel, where 'one could sit for hours, watching the light & shades playing about the hills & waters & the constant panorama going on below.'[18]

They arrived in Ottawa on the 25th of September. Lady Aberdeen's notes on her initial reactions to Rideau Hall are intensely characteristic of her rapid and discursive style:

It was a bright morning & H. D. [Henry Drummond] & I ransacked all over the premises & grounds & inspected skating rinks, toboggan slides, curling rinks, etc., etc. The servants' departments are very ample & very comfortably ar-

plate 136

plate 137

January they launched a fire balloon which sailed dangerously off over the treetops. They presented two plays that year, Archie taking the title role in *David Copperfield* (Plate 134) and that of Mrs Bennet in *Pride and Prejudice* (Plate 135). At about this time the permanent stage was replaced with moveable panels so that the space could be used as an extension of the ballroom.[39]

Charitable works were afoot. Lady Aberdeen was behind the founding of a local council of women and of University Extension lectures in Ottawa, but plans for a public library failed to materialize (see page 116). Far from being exclusively Presbyterian, Protestant, or even Christian in her sympathies, she welcomed the pleaders of many causes, including Dr Wilfred Grenfell of the Labrador Mission, Father Albert Lacombe, the apostle of the western Indians, and the wife of the Chief Rabbi. She was appalled by the regional and denominational divisions in Canadian society, but her strenuous efforts to overcome them often had only the immediate effect of eliciting protests from both sides of any given question—from Protestants *and* Catholics, or from Temperance ladies *and* the easier-going members of society.[40] But against all odds the

Aberdeens kept up the fight, and the country benefited in the end. Only a governor-general and his wife could even have attempted what they did.

In order to reach out into the life of the country they paid extended visits to provincial capitals and the larger cities. In January 1894 they attended the winter carnival in Quebec, where Lady Aberdeen was delighted to see ice statues of Champlain, Laval, and de Salaberry and remarked on the mutual courtesy displayed by citizens of both languages. On a similar visit to Toronto they visited the colleges of the University. One young student acted as their aide-de-camp for the day and wrote in his diary:

I showed them into their carriage then I ran along side it & talked to the Governor General and Lady Aberdeen all the way to Victoria College. I enjoyed the conversation with them very much.

MacGregor Dawson has noted this as an early example of Mackenzie King's[41] uncanny talent for making contacts; it was also the beginning of a long friendship.

In the late winter the household was saddened by the death of Lady

Aberdeen's father. All engagements were postponed and Government House servants were put into 'mourning liveries.'[42] In March, after the opening of Parliament, came the first annual meeting of the National Council of Women. By this time the French-speaking Catholic, the Jewish, and the Unitarian ladies were joining up, and a deadlock loomed over the form of prayer with which meetings should open. This was resolved when Lady Aberdeen's friend, Mrs Emily Cummings, a Toronto newspaperwoman, had the inspiration to suggest silent prayer.[43]

In May the house was restored to its customary bustle by a series of garden-parties. At the first of these Lady Aberdeen noted:

There was some doubt as to the dress for gentlemen & whether top-hats & frock coats were *de rigueur*. We advocated flannels & tennis, cricket (Plate 136) & croquet—& so there will be no difficulty as to this next time.[44]

The six parliamentary dinners that season posed the problem of seating the ladies at predominantly male gatherings, Lady Aberdeen reporting that some of the seventy-odd guests had to be content with A.D.C.s sitting between them.[45] At this point Aberdeen's portrait (Plate 137) was being painted by Robert Harris of *Fathers of Confederation* fame.[46] His wife laid the corner-stone of the Ottawa Y.W.C.A. which she had helped to found. And they held a garden-party for the Royal Society, at which, oddly enough for the nature of the gathering, the main attraction was a troupe of performing dogs.

Lady Aberdeen spent the early part of the summer in England, her husband remaining in Canada as he always did in those politically troubled years. Later in the season they made their first tour of the Maritime Provinces. At Halifax they found the Public Gardens planted in the form of the Aberdeen arms; at Charlottetown they admired 'nice old fashioned' Government House[47] with its fine view of the harbour; at Saint John Lady Aberdeen attended a council of women; and at Fredericton they found the Anglican bishop sighing 'for the flesh pots of England.'[48] Then, in an interval at Quebec, they spent a day at St Anne-de-Beaupré. Lady Aberdeen described the shrine most sympathetically but was not so tolerant of a Presbyterian sermon in Quebec on the conversion of the French: 'If only they would make the Protestants *Christians* & as moral as the R.C.s they would advance their cause quicker!'[49]

By late summer they were in railway carriage *Victoria* making their first tour of the west (Plate 138). This included a week at Government House, Winnipeg (Plate 120) and shorter stops along the way. At Edmonton they drove out to see Father Lacombe's mission at St Albert. In British Columbia they found the Guisachan fruit a failure but Coldstream and its new jam factory prospering. Finally, in that 'decidedly English'[50] capital Victoria, Lady Aberdeen formed yet another council of women.

On the return journey in November they stopped at Montreal and borrowed the late Sir John Abbott's house for a few days. Characteristically, Lady Aberdeen noted in her diary that 'It *looked* very clean . . . but when they came to look *under* the carpets, it was another matter.' She was overwhelmed by the central heating and decided that it was this feature of North American life that accounted for 'the pastiness & delicacy of the majority of the women.'[51] One evening after dinner she admired Sir William Van Horne's collection of Japanese pottery and paintings by Corot and Monticelli.[52]

plate 138

plate 144

plate 145

On the 27th Bowell finally resigned, and the elder Tupper formed a government. An election was called for the 23rd of June.

By then the Aberdeens were in Quebec, where at lilac time it was 'so homy looking—so different from Ottawa.'[74] The election returns, as they came in, were flashed on a screen on Dufferin Terrace. Tupper, though he lost the election, yet pressed for the appointment of senators and judges. In denying him these, Aberdeen drew down on himself the fury of both Tuppers.[75] Lady Aberdeen was cut to the quick by the severance of her friendship with the Hibbert Tuppers. In early July the Prime Minister, 'the plucky old thing,'[76] came to Government House to resign. Laurier formed a government.

Later in July the Aberdeens went to the Gaspé where they had bought Stanley House. Lady Aberdeen, intrigued by the Canadian passion for passing the summer within bare wooden walls, did nothing to the house except to varnish the interior.[77]

After the opening of the new Parliament in August they visited a series of Ontario fall fairs. These innocent affairs were not without their hazards. At Peterborough a platform collapsed, and in another town the mayor introduced a uniformed A.D.C. as the Governor-General. At the Toronto Exhibition they were treated to a grand-stand show of performing elephants and a simulated storming of the Bastille.

That Christmas, after a visit to Coldstream Ranch, they sent out three thousand Christmas cards, a thousand more than previously, prepared by Topley the photographer. As gifts they gave baskets of roses and Scottish white heather to the ladies and buttonholes to their husbands.

Early in the new year, 1897, minor changes were made to the house. The ballroom was enriched with gilt cornices[78] (Plate 146). The upper room of the curling rink was painted red, decorated with moose heads, and furnished with Turkey-red settees in an attempt to create a Canadian atmosphere.[79] At this time too Lady Aberdeen received several visits from Ottawa's eccentric new mayor, Samuel Bingham, who appeared on one occasion bewigged in a carriage and on another in a blanket coat and on snowshoes.[80]

In honour of Queen Victoria's Diamond Jubilee in 1897 Lady Aberdeen pressed with all her might for the establishment of the Victorian Order of Nurses, dedicated to the care of the sick in their own homes. This noble female organization, mistrusted at first by the doctors, was to be her greatest monument. She also promoted Indian Famine Relief, a club for news-boys, prison reform, and other modern-sounding social projects.

After witnessing the West Block fire on Parliament Hill, attending her brother's wedding in Nashville, inspecting the new Library of

plate 146

plate 147

Congress in Washington, and seeing a demonstration of the cinemato-graph in New York, Lady Aberdeen received an honorary degree from the University of Chicago for all her mighty works. That she was the first woman to address Convocation, and that she should do so on All Fools' Day tickled her sense of humour.[81] Another degree came from Queen's University, Kingston, where the students gave their 'yell:' 'What's the matter with Lady Aberdeen?' and the response, 'She's all right, you bet!'[82]

In May the Aberdeens went to Quebec to inspect the Jubilee contingent of troops leaving for England. These included the North West Mounted Police, who were to create a sensation in London. So was Sir Wilfrid Laurier, who had reluctantly accepted the knighthood proposed by Aberdeen and Sir Donald Smith.

Lady Aberdeen, meanwhile, after attending the Jubilee celebration in Halifax, departed for England and visited Gladstone for the last time before his death. On her return she and her husband attended the meetings of the British Association in Toronto, where they met the great scientists Lister and Kelvin. She describes a reception held at

The Grange:

Yes the Goldwin Smiths! Who would have thought that the day would come when H. E. & Goldwin Smith would have been seen hobnobbing together, & H. E. drinking his host's health in a silver gobblet [*sic.*] belonging to the first Governor of Ontario. It is a curious fact that the man who has been preaching annexation as the true destiny of Canada in season & out of season, & who has written contemptuously of the various ceremonials in connection with the Vice-Regal Court, should also be the man to receive us in the most absolute royal manner, every point of étiquette being most formally observed—special gate reserved for our carriage alone to enter, band ready to strike up the moment we appeared—red cloth—the Goldwin Smiths themselves on doorsteps & hat in hand—all the time ready to fetch anybody we wanted to speak to. It was all very funny.[83]

In October there was another tour of the east, with Charles Moss in attendance to record the scenery. The party observed the Highland settlements on Cape Breton Island, were charmed by Sackville and its little university, and attended Victorian Order of Nurses meetings at Saint John. Then Aberdeen went to receive an honorary degree at Princeton, where they met Woodrow Wilson. On the way home they stopped at 'dear beautiful Boston'[84] to seek out Dr Alfred Worcester[85] and inspect his celebrated training school for nurses at Waltham.

plate 148

plate 149

In November Lady Aberdeen recorded a major triumph. The medical profession of Ottawa had approved the V.O.N.! She had invited them to Rideau Hall for a meeting with Worcester, and in their astonishment that such a militant lady could provide them with suitable refreshments, they had allowed the American to win them over after only seven hours.[86] It was not so easy at a similar meeting in Toronto where, as she noted, 'Society was dead against us.'[87] Nothing daunted, she again brought her Boston friend into the fray. He, after one of his hostile audience taunted him by asking how much the Aberdeens paid him to do their work, turned the tables by hinting that opposition to the V.O.N. implied disloyalty to the Queen whose name it bore. This was too much for Toronto, and the day was won[88] (Plate 147).

At about this time a delegation of Ottawa cabmen protested the extension of the tram-lines to the gates of Rideau Hall, which the Aberdeens had desired in order to bring more people in. The better folk muttered that Government House was becoming more than ever a resort for all and sundry. Gossip throve on highly exaggerated accounts of the Household Club such as are reflected in a letter Lord Minto wrote to his brother soon after arriving in 1898:

The establishment was too awful—punctuality for anything unknown—dinner sometimes not till 10 p.m. His A.D.C.s starving, and picking up what they could. He wandering about the house at night, and always having something to eat at 2 a.m., never down till 10.30 a.m. or 11 a.m., before which he had to be fed several times. . . . The Haddo Club (or terms of equality with the servants every Thursday night) when subjects were brought forward for discussion, in which I hear on one occasion the butler considerably bested H. E.—the servants consequently odious to everyone. . . . She had a great many people by the ears. She went in for everything she cd. think of and invented other things to go in for. . . . They absolutely upset society.[89]

There was some justice in the last remark. The Aberdeens' work might have been more effective had it been done more subtly.

The great event that autumn was the Victorian Era Ball[90] (Plate 148) which Lady Aberdeen arranged in the Toronto Armouries to stimulate patriotism and foster unity. It included massive processions heralded by trumpeters, dances accompanied by bands, and heavy agricultural machinery rollicking about the vast hall. Also on the programme were *tableaux vivants* of famous Victorian paintings such as *The Huguenot* by Millais, *Napoleon and Madame Récamier* by Orchardson, and *Car-*

plate 150

plate 151

mencita by Sargent. All Toronto was present at this loyal demonstration and was obliged to acknowledge its debt to Lady Aberdeen.

She and her husband returned to Ottawa for New Year's Day 1898. This last year of their stay was marked by strenuous efforts to get the V.O.N. on its feet. It also saw bitter attacks on the Aberdeens by the elder Tupper. He refused to dine at Government House and returned the gift the Aberdeens sent him and his wife on their golden wedding anniversary.

Entertaining continued unabated. Yet another programme of historical tableaux was presented, this time in Montreal. In the spring a novel venture was launched in the form of the 'May Queen's Court of Ottawa,' a garden-party of young women held at Rideau Hall in aid of hospitals.[91] But in the midst of it all Lady Aberdeen complained of poor old Rideau Hall:

It is a pity that Govt. House entertaining cannot be made more useful in mixing people up & in giving opportunities for politicians to meet on neutral ground. But its distance from the town is against all that & it has never been the custom.[92]

They did little on the whole to change the house. Its state is recorded in an article, by Florence Hamilton Randal of the Ottawa *Journal*, in the *Canadian Magazine* for November 1898:

On entering the Hall two flights of stairs ascend (Plates 149, 150). The one on the left leads to the Ball Room, the beauty of its white and gold mouldings and cornices striking the eye at first glance. . . . On great occasions there is set up the the dais or throne, over which hangs the oil painting of Lord Aberdeen done by Robert Harris. . . . In some of the rooms upstairs the carpets look decidedly the worse for wear. The corridors are the most striking feature. The lobby narrows into one long aisle connecting the old part with the new; turning to the left by the conservatory it ends in the Chapel.

Her Ladyship's boudoir or study (Plate 151), that of His Excellency, and the drawing room form a suite of rooms in which the colour scheme is the same. They are carpeted in the crimson brussels used in the corridors; the paper is of pale green. . . . Pale green chintz covers the furniture. . . . In Lady Aberdeen's study are several good pictures. . . . A grandfather's clock is in the room, and Gladstone's face looks down benignly from the wall. . . . Those who are invited to dinner at Government House dine in a room that can seat thirty. The ceiling and walls are tinted in terra cotta, the mouldings being of black and gold. A stuffed bear stands in one corner, a memento of the Quebec Carnival.[93]

By the summer the Aberdeens' period was nearing its end (Plate 152). With the Tuppers declining any part in the farewell addresses,[94] Parliament presented them with a dinner service hand-painted with Canadian scenes. After final visits to British Columbia and the Gaspé, Aberdeen unveiled the Champlain monument on Dufferin Terrace, Quebec. In

October there was the farewell dinner at Rideau Hall and the closing service in the chapel, at which 'God be with you till we meet again' was tearfully sung. As a final gesture Aberdeen presented the chapel to the government. Unfortunately it was little appreciated by his successors and was eventually dismantled and sent to a mission district.[95]

In their last weeks the Aberdeens discussed with Laurier the improvement of Ottawa. Lady Aberdeen urged a new Government House nearer to town; but dearer to the Prime Minister's heart was a general scheme comprising a 'stately drive' along Sussex Street, a park on Nepean Point, a bridge to the Gatineau, and a geological museum.[96] All these have long since come into being, but Government House fortunately remains at historic Rideau Hall. In the end even Lady Aberdeen had to admit a 'sneaking fondness' for Ottawa (Plate 153), 'in spite of its shabby old Government House put away amongst its clump of bushes & in spite of dirty old tumble down Sussex Street'.[97]

The farewells continued. In early November a subscription banquet costing $11 a plate was held for them in Toronto. The menu, comparatively modest for the nineties, is preserved in the Aberdeen papers:

Oysters in aspic
Consommé Victoria
Lobster à la Newburg
Lamb Chops à l'Ambassadrice
Timbales of Chicken Lord Aberdeen
PUNCH
Suprême of Wild Duck
Salad Waldorf
Surprise
Cream of Gingembre
Coffee[98]

Faithful to tradition, they departed from Quebec, but not until Lady Aberdeen had noted some improvements that had been made to the Citadel. The worst of the rooms had been repainted and new matting laid—this latter indicating that the house was still regarded as a camping-out place—but the 'horrible' old brown paper in the drawing-room remained, and 'a proper overhaul of all the sanitary arrangements'[99] was overdue. They sailed on the 12th of November after having witnessed Lord Minto's swearing-in.

This was far from being the end of their careers. Aberdeen became Lord Lieutenant of Ireland a second time in 1906, and his wife again worked furiously for a multitude of Irish causes, especially public health. In 1915, the year after they left Dublin, he was advanced to Marquess of Aberdeen and Temair. She continued as president of the International Council of Women for many years and travelled very widely. She turned up at Rideau Hall almost as regularly as when she was 'governess general.'[100]

A turning point in their lives came when Archie was killed in a motor accident in 1909,[101] and as the years of their retirement wore on they took comfort in spiritualism.[102] They kept up their friendships with many Canadians, especially Laurier until his death, and Mackenzie King[103] until Lord Aberdeen's death in 1934 and Lady Aberdeen's in 1939.

plate 153

plate 154

CHAPTER FIVE / *A NEW CENTURY*

Lord Minto and Lord Grey, at the turn of the century, saw great changes take place in Canada. Following upon the economic depressions of the nineteenth century, their period was one of prosperity and expansion, of immigration on a large scale and an optimistic Canadianism of which Sir Wilfrid Laurier was the presiding genius. The movement towards Imperial Unity, which had gained momentum in England during the race for overseas territory, strongly coloured the activities of both these governors-general. Lord Grey in particular represented the extreme attitude that is reflected in one of his utterances, 'The British Empire appears to me to be the religion of righteousness itself.'[1] Yet both these men, like so many of their predecessors, became astonishingly Canadian.

It was, in fact, the confluence of national and Imperial enthusiasms, which they embodied in themselves, that lent their period its special flavour. Another ingredient was the ebullient spirit of the Edwardian period, which with the accompanying reaction to late Victorianism, had its echoes at Rideau Hall.

Gilbert John Elliot, 4th Earl of Minto (1854-1914)[2] (Plate 154) had already served in Canada as military secretary to Lord Lansdowne and as chief of staff to General Middleton during the second Riel Rebellion. Sir John Macdonald's prophecy in 1886 that Canada would some day welcome him back as Governor-General[3] came true only twelve years after it was made.

Born in London the great-grandson of a governor of Bengal, he had spent his boyhood at Minto House in Roxboroughshire and assumed the courtesy title of Lord Melgund when his father succeeded to the

plate 155

plate 156

earldom in 1859. After Eton and Cambridge he became a celebrated gentleman-jockey and enjoyed the distinction of having broken his neck and living to tell the tale. As a young officer, he observed wars in Europe and the East before taking up his first Canadian post in 1883. The years of Gladstonian Liberalism—anathema to him—he spent at home occupying himself with sport, landscape gardening, and the family archives. He succeeded to the peerage in 1891. His wife Mary (Plate 155) was the charming and clever sister of Lord Grey. On the eve of their departure for Canada in 1898 the aged Queen, doubtless with the example of Lady Aberdeen fresh in her mind, offered Lady Minto some royal advice:

You must never be persuaded to give your name to any new venture which might be criticized. Your dear father advised me to make this rule nearly forty years ago and I have never deviated from it.[4]

Minto was a solid and straightforward man who has been unjustly regarded as 'wooden'[5] and as 'less . . . Governor General than . . . Imperial Commissioner.'[6] The first accusation is patently untrue. As for the second, Laurier's assessment of Minto as the most constitutional governor he had known[7] has been borne out in recent studies.[8]

The Mintos arrived in Quebec in November 1898 with five children ranging in age from two to fourteen: Esmond, Larry Lord Melgund, Violet, Ruby, and Eileen; the Military Secretary, Major Laurence Drummond;[9] two aides-de-camp, Captain A. C. Bell[10] and Captain Harry Graham,[11] comic writer and lyricist; and a comptroller, Arthur Guise (Plate 156). Lord Aberdeen, as has been noted, witnessed the swearing-in, and Lady Aberdeen handed over to Lady Minto a bulky portfolio of charities.

Minto has already been heard on the subject of the Aberdeen house-

plate 168

long as anyone could remember, and the accession of Edward VII. Unfortunately, the memorial service which Minto arranged at Christ Church Cathedral became the cause of complaint by those who felt that he was acting as if the Church of England were established in Canada.[39] A new Military Secretary, Captain Stanley Maude,[40] now arrived to replace Drummond. At the same time the assiduous Mackenzie King appeared on the scene as a filler of gaps at the dinner table (Plates 167, 168). Though the young deputy minister found the Minto girls 'bright and natural,' he reproached himself in his diary after each visit for having indulged in 'small talk.'[41]

The greatest event of the period took place in 1901. A month before her death Queen Victoria had authorized the extension of the Australian voyage of her grandson and his wife, the Duke and Duchess of Cornwall and York*, to include Canada.

This, Prince George's third visit to Canada, and the first major royal tour since that of his father in 1860, is amply documented in a souvenir volume[42] by Joseph Pope, one of its principal arrangers. My illustrations come from this book and from Queen Mary's photograph albums at Windsor.

The royal party of twenty-two, which included the Duchess's brother, Prince Alexander of Teck (later Earl of Athlone), a private chaplain, and two artists, landed at Quebec on the 16th of September. Here the Duke received the first of many loyal addresses, reviewed the first of many troops, and accepted from Laval his first honorary degree. One

*The official title of Prince George (later King George V) from January to November 1901; in the latter month he became Prince of Wales.

plate 170

plate 169

plate 171

plate 172

evening after dinner at the Citadel, which had recently been overhauled by Lady Minto,[43] the party heard a concert on Dufferin Terrace and watched a display of fireworks which culminated in an immense portrait of the Duke.

The Canadian Pacific Railway for the occasion had built two new railway carriages (Plates 169, 170) which were modestly described as 'the most splendid ever constructed.'[44] They were equipped with electric lights and internal telephones. In the day car *Cornwall* was a reception-room panelled in Circassian walnut with blue and gold Louis-Quinze ornament and a piano. Its dining-room was painted in the style of Watteau. Car *York* contained the bedrooms. The entire royal train had ten cars in all.

Montreal was its first stop. Here the separate English and French reception committees had caused a little preliminary confusion. The royal couple stayed at Lord Strathcona's house, and Minto had qualms about their host 'trying to lead society . . . with a squaw for a wife who is absolutely hopeless.'[45] But everything went off perfectly, with torchlight processions through the city, fireworks blazing from the Mountain, and receptions at both universities.

Ottawa's turn came next. After their arrival at the Elgin Street station the Duke and Duchess were received (Plate 171) in a 'royal pavilion' on Parliament Hill before driving to Rideau Hall (Plate 172), which had been much refurbished on their account.[46] Pope notes the 'uniform affability, consideration and kindness'[47] of the Duchess; and we know from James Pope-Hennessey's recent biography of Queen Mary that this remarkable woman was only then conquering her shyness and

plate 173

plate 174

110

plate 175

emerging as a tower of strength to her husband.[48] A lacrosse match for the Minto Cup so pleased the Duke that he kept the ball that was used. Then came the unveiling of Philippe Hébert's monument to Queen Victoria. But the real novelty among their various entertainments was a trip down the timber slide at the Chaudière (Plate 173), followed by canoe races and a picnic in the Rockcliffe woods.[49] Here the lumbermen of the region had built a shanty, and they treated the royal pair to a demonstration of tree-felling and dancing and to a luncheon of pork and beans (Plate 174).

For the tour of the west Minto tactfully stayed behind in order to allow full scope to the lieutenant-governors of the provinces,[50] but his wife and Household and the Prime Minister followed in their own train. At Government House, Winnipeg (Plates 120, 175) luncheon was 'admirably served,'[51] and afterwards the Duke opened the new science building at the University of Manitoba. At Calgary there was the usual parley with the Indians and an exhibition of rough-riding.

On reaching Vancouver at the end of September the royal couple appeared before massed school children in Stanley Park. Then, in Victoria, after seeing Chinatown and receiving gifts of Indian crafts, they began the return journey. This was broken at Banff where the Duchess drove out to see Tunnel Mountain, the hot springs, and Lake Louise (Plate 176, 177), and acquired four of Frederic Bell-Smith's

plate 176

plate 177

112

western sketches. A special train took the Duke and Prince Alexander to Poplar Point, Manitoba, where Minto joined them for a few days' duck shooting (Plate 178)—a part of the tour which had required some little persuasion on Minto's part for the government to arrange.[52]

The two parties were reunited on their visit to Toronto. Arriving on the 10th of October to the strains of a musical welcome by the Mendelssohn Choir, they drove through elaborately decorated streets and under several welcome arches (Plate 179) to old Government House in King Street (Plate 180). One evening they heard the famous French singer Emma Calvé at Massey Hall. After Toronto came short visits to other towns including London, Niagara (Plate 181), Hamilton, Kingston, and Montreal (where the Duke opened the rebuilt Victoria Bridge).

The tour ended with visits to Saint John and Halifax and a final day in Newfoundland. The whole affair, in Minto's words, had been 'a triumphant display of loyal sentiment.'[53] In making the arrangements he had accurately gauged the temper of the public, who particularly appreciated the innovation of royalty shaking hands with them.[54]

In 1902 the Mintos attended the coronation of Edward VII in London, and at this time we begin to hear a good deal about Imperial Unity. Lord Grey wrote to Minto rejoicing in the selection of a Canadian enthusiast, George Parkin, as secretary of the Rhodes Scholarships.[55] But for all this Minto was genuinely concerned with national unity and shrewd enough to understand the French-speaking element's lack of instinctive response to the mystique of Anglo-Saxonism.[56] In an attempt to overcome the cleavage between the two sections of the population he held special functions in Montreal, for which he borrowed Lord Strathcona's house for days at a time.[57]

Sport continued to occupy his leisure time. He fished at Lake St John, shot duck at Long Point and moose on the Ottawa, and fox-hunted at St Anne's. He survived a fall from his horse and narrowly escaped drowning while walking on the frozen Ottawa.[58] His children were keen horsemen, though Ruby also did well in her music and Eileen in her acting. They all took part in a performance of *Alice in Wonderland* at a fancy-dress ball at Christmas 1902.[59]

By 1903 Minto was thinking of the end of his term and of his prospects for India, when Joseph Chamberlain persuaded him to stay another year.[60] Lady Minto, between trips to Washington, Newport, and Japan, was being painted by Robert Harris[61] who, with Hébert the sculptor,

plate 178

plate 179

113

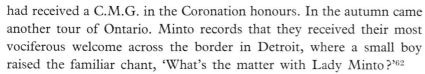

plate 180

plate 181

had received a C.M.G. in the Coronation honours. In the autumn came another tour of Ontario. Minto records that they received their most vociferous welcome across the border in Detroit, where a small boy raised the familiar chant, 'What's the matter with Lady Minto?'[62]

In matters political, a crisis arose over the new officer commanding the Militia, Lord Dundonald, who made public criticism of his Minister —and like his predecessor was recalled to England.[63] Reciprocity with the United States Minto regarded as a distinct threat to Imperial Unity;[64] but the debate over this question went on long after his departure. Meanwhile his concern for American influence in Canada extended to such details as American flags flying over summer cottages in Muskoka.[65] In order to interest Canadians in their own country and its history he successfully urged a proper building for the Public Archives.[66]

Yet early in 1904, with Lady Minto suffering the effects of 'Xmas trees & children's parties,' the house was 'flooded with visitors from N. York and Montreal.'[67] It is interesting to observe the ambivalence of the Imperialist attitude towards things American. On the one hand resisting specific influences, on the other they were anxious to 'clean the slate' between England and America and achieve a grand union of all Anglo-Saxons.

Disaster followed disaster in the spring. Lady Minto broke a leg while skating. Then, on Easter Day, while she was still confined to bed, a fire broke out in the Minto Wing next to her room, and she was carried out on a folding screen. The new wing was gutted, and the Governor-General's study and his wife's sitting-room downstairs were damaged by water. The entire household were crammed into the west wing of the house for the rest of their stay.[68]

The last of their functions in Ottawa (Plates 182, 183) took place in August. At the conclusion of a farewell tour of the west Lord Grey's appointment was announced. On the eve of their departure from Quebec in November, Minto sent a parting gift to his 'very true friend'[69] Sir Wilfrid Laurier.

Minto's later life is too well known from John Buchan's biography[70] to need retelling here. In 1905 he succeeded Curzon as Viceroy of India, and his period was marked by important reforms in government. He retired to England in 1910 and died in 1914.

Lord Grey (Plate 184) was by all counts the most colourful figure at Rideau Hall since Dufferin. He was certainly its most fulsome speaker,[71] though this to one of his critics, John Morley, was no asset:

Have we sent you [he asked Goldwin Smith] a sufficiently superb windbag to rule over you in Ottawa? I thought grimly of you as I read his flummery in the *Times* to-day. I hope Laurier will keep H.E.'s claws clipped.[72]

Laurier had his work cut out for him. Grey, backed up by powerful friends from the King to the American industrial barons, bombarded his long-suffering Prime Minister with suggestions nearly every day of his term, which was the longest of any governor-general since Confederation.

Albert Edward, 4th Earl Grey (1851-1917),[73] a grandson of the Grey of Reform Bill fame, was born at St James's Palace while his father was private secretary to Prince Albert. The Prince of Wales acknowledged him as a 'friend from earliest childhood,'[74] and in fact he had accompanied the Prince on an early trip to India, where it was that Grey lost his hair after a sunstroke. He began public life as a Liberal member of Parliament, breaking with the party over Home Rule; but his real call to duty came through the influence of Toynbee and a study of the life of Mazzini. Though his wide interests embraced agriculture, travel, sport, and social reform, he fixed on Imperial Unity as his main cause after a meeting with Cecil Rhodes. His wife Alice (Plate 185) was a daughter of the art collector Robert Holford of Dorchester House.

In Canada Grey found full scope for his Imperial zeal, his oratory, and his charm with people. Laurier testified that he gave 'his whole heart, his whole soul, and his whole life to Canada.'[75] In a period of material prosperity he became not only the country's best advertising agent but its spur in the pursuit of higher things.

Immediately upon arrival at Quebec late in 1904 he espoused the cause, a favourite of all governors-general since Dufferin, of the preservation of the walls and battlefields.[76] Success in this was to come in his time. In Ottawa, his first act was somewhat less significant but not without symbolic value: facing-off the puck in a hockey match between Ottawa and Dawson City.[77]

It is impossible in a small space to mention but a few of Grey's many activities. His travels began early in 1905 with official visits to Quebec and Montreal. Of the latter city he remarked, 'The English people of Montreal would be much gayer & happier & cultured if they allowed a little French sunlight to warm and illuminate their lives.'[78] In the spring he paid his first visit to the United States, choosing West Point[79] as (probably) for him one of the best American institutions. Visitors from both Europe and America began to appear in numbers at Rideau Hall

plate 182

plate 183

115

plate 184

and the Citadel: Sarah Bernhardt, Admiral Prince Louis of Battenberg, Andrew Carnegie (who opened the Ottawa Public Library),[80] and Violet Markham the labour writer (who first met her lifelong friend Mackenzie King at a torchlight skating party).[81]

Grey found his travels in Canada immensely stimulating. In the

plate 185

summer of 1905 he visited Toronto and fished at Anticosti and the Gaspé before taking up residence at the Citadel, writing furiously to Laurier all the while to propose all sorts of schemes: lantern lectures on the Empire, the restoration of Louisbourg,[82] a great hotel for Ottawa[83] —the germinal idea of the Château Laurier—and the designation 'Royal' for hotels and clubs in order to keep the monarchy before the eyes of Canadians.[84] Most important was his journey west to inaugurate the new provinces of Saskatchewan and Alberta, each one 'a new leaf to Your Majesty's Maple Crown,' as he telegraphed to the King.[85] His speech at Edmonton is a further example of his mode of expression:

The day which marks the addition of a new self-governing province to the Dominion, and thus to the galaxy of self-governing states whose combined brilliancy makes the constellation of the British Empire the brightest the world has ever seen, is a red letter day in the history of the Empire. That the Province of Alberta will bring, in ever-increasing measure as time goes on, strength and

plate 186

lustre to the British Crown, and prove worthy of the illustrious prince whose name it is its honour to bear,[86] is both my sanguine hope and confident expectation.[87]

In Winnipeg he urged the citizens to have 'the best schools, the best churches, the best music, the best art, the best newspapers and the best literature in the Dominion.'[88] In even more prophetic vein at the Manitoba Club he foresaw the province assuming 'the proportions of a gigantic colossus, ministering with one hand to the needs of Europe and with the other to those of Asia.'[89] In view of such utterances as these it is no wonder that every town in the country clamoured for a visit from the Governor-General.[90]

Meanwhile, at Rideau Hall, the Minto Wing had been repaired (Plate 186) and the Household were settling in. The Secretary at Rideau Cottage (Plate 187) (which was now being enlarged at the back)[91] was Colonel John Hanbury-Williams.[92] The aides-de-camp formed a somewhat grander collection than previously, including Lord Bury (later Lord Albemarle who revisited Rideau Hall in 1965), Lord Lascelles (later Lord Harewood, and Princess Mary's husband), and Lord Alan Percy (later Duke of Northumberland). Grey's daughters Evelyn and Sybil[92a] acted as ladies-in-waiting to their mother.

Social functions followed the established pattern of past years, as is evident in a contemporary account of the house:

Whilst the tone and colour of entertainments may differ, one can easily mention a list of gaieties almost sure to come off at Government House—a couple of dances at Christmas, musicales in Lent, skating and tobogganing every Saturday afternoon during the winter, with moonlight parties of the same description thrown in. Dinners are given frequently, especially during the session of Parliament, a State Ball is held after Easter and several garden parties in the early summer.

The present Governor-General is striving to make the interior of the Vice-Regal residence artistically handsome as well as serviceable, and to form therein the nucleus of a portrait gallery. . . . The conservatories are very fine and are the especial care of Her Excellency[93] the Countess Grey.[94]

The portraits which Grey was acquiring included those of Edward VII and Queen Alexandra, Durham, Elgin, Dufferin, and Stanley, which are still in the house.[95] Lady Grey had masses of daffodils planted in the grounds and sponsored garden competitions in Ottawa.

Sport maintained its place of honour. The Grey Cup for football (Plate 188) still keeps its donor's memory green. Hockey was attracting more and more attention, and skating and curling continued in full force at Rideau Hall (Plate 189).

In 1906 another addition was made to the house. The Governor-

117

plate 187

plate 188

plate 189

General's study[96] at the far end of the 1865 wing—'a room literally full of warm brilliant sunshine,'[97] as Grey described it—was designed to repeat the form of Thomas MacKay's curved gable of 1838 (Plates 186, 190). This, with the new greenhouse behind the Minto Wing,[98] gave the garden side of the house its present-day appearance, except that the verandas have since been removed.

At this time Grey in his turn was requesting more salary, pleading that he was spending $20,000 above his statutory amount, much of it in travelling.[99] Thus early in 1906 he attended a Pilgrims' dinner in New York,[100] at the same time holding private talks with President Theodore Roosevelt.[101] In May and June he toured Ontario, commenting on each town's special feature in characteristic language. In Toronto it was the lake shore, 'that beautiful Mediterranean Sea,' and in Hamilton the

plate 190

plate 191

'Table Mountain and its Bay of Naples.'[102] Just the sort of thing these cities loved to hear!

It was, however, in British Columbia that his enthusiasm reached its peak. Speaking before the Canadian Club of Vancouver, he conjured up visions of an international fruit industry; and he wrote to Laurier about the export of electric power to the United States.[103] Here as elsewhere he gave evidence of an uncanny ability to appeal to business men, making each one feel like a pioneer, statesman, and missionary rolled into one. Finally, after a visit to Newfoundland, he declared himself in favour of its annexation to Canada as well as that of Saint-Pierre and Miquelon, Bermuda, and the West Indies.[104]

He was just as energetic in his promotion of cultural matters. He arranged music and drama festivals and had Hébert make trophies

(Plate 191) for the competitions.[105] His personal interest in the National Gallery led directly to its severance from the Royal Canadian Academy and to the formation of its permanent collection.[106] As early as December 1906 he began his major task of organizing the Quebec Tercentenary with the purpose of 'harmonizing and unifying the two great races which together make the Nation of Canada' and of promoting Imperial Unity.[107]

In the following year, 1907, though saddened by the death of a daughter in England, he eagerly pursued his many activities. The discussions on church union in Canada[108] interested him, not that he held any formal beliefs himself but that he felt a larger body could better promote national and Imperial feeling. His guests were as varied as ever: General Booth of the Salvation Army (Plate 192); Elihu Root, Roosevelt's secretary of state, and Lord Bryce, the British ambassador

119

plate 192

to Washington; Rudyard Kipling and Ernest Thompson Seton; the Lord Chancellor of England and the Bishop of London. In the spring he attended the Carnegie Peace Congress in New York[109] and studied the battlefields at Gettysburg in order to gather ideas for Quebec. In May he engaged Stephen Leacock to make a tour of the Empire lecturing on Imperial organization.[110]

The first important visit to Canada of foreign royalty took place that summer of 1907. It was doubtless in preparation for the arrival of Prince Fushima of Japan that the drawing-rooms and dining-room of Rideau Hall were 'Georgianized' by the addition of new mouldings and chimney-pieces to replace the old Victorian ones.[111] At a garden-party for the Prince the grounds were decked out with Japanese lanterns (Plate 193), and a visit to the Dominion Experimental Farm was described by the Governor-General.

I selected a young maple, recently planted, in a commanding position, and asked him if he would allow the tree to have the honour of being associated with his name. He descended from our motor, walked round the tree, bowed to it, and ex-

pressed himself delighted at the suggestion that the tree should be known as Prince Fushima's tree.[112]

The lacquer box and the $1,000 for charity which the Prince gave to Lady Grey on his departure[113] were highly acceptable, but Grey was annoyed that the Prince should have distributed medals to butlers and coachmen.[114]

In July he made another tour of the Maritime Provinces, explaining that 'every province in turn had captured his heart.'[115] Here as elsewhere he coined a new slogan for each town and left 'a new scheme on every doorstep.'[116]

The next year, 1908, saw Laurier's re-election and Grey's active sponsorship of Mackenzie King. Perceiving in the young man who was helping Evelyn with her lectures to working girls a future prime minister of Canada, he successfully urged his appointment to a Royal Commission on Laurier.[117] Among the Governor-General's other causes were the introduction of reindeer into Labrador,[118] a tuberculosis campaign,[119] Civil Service reform,[120] and a winter carnival for Montreal. In the latter project he encountered a curious Canadian prejudice:

It appears to me [he wrote to Laurier] that it is mistaken tactics to be ashamed of your winter, and try to conceal it. To glorify it, and to pity those unfortunate countries which are not blessed with our winter sports and exhilerating [sic.] winter weather is I believe the right, and in the long run, the winning attitude.[121]

One of his visitors that year was the popular English novelist Mrs Humphrey Ward, who became quite captivated with Lord Grey before setting out to tour the west in Sir William Van Horne's private railway car.[122] The resulting novel, *Lady Merton, Colonist*,[123] includes a meeting with a governor-general on the station platform in Winnipeg ('We always seem to send the right man') and has as its hero an idealistic young politician evidently modelled on Mackenzie King.

The greatest event of 1908, and indeed of Grey's whole period, was the Quebec Tercentenary celebration,[124] for which he had toiled long and hard. In the face of opposition from what he called 'the curés'[125] (the ultramontane and anti-imperial section of Canadian opinion) he had set up an Empire-wide fund to purchase the Plains of Abraham. By the spring of 1908 the Battlefields Commission was appointed and rehearsals had begun for elaborate pageants (Plates 194, 195) re-enacting the early history of Quebec. In July the descendants of Montcalm, Lévis, and Murray arrived as guests of the government. But the crowning

plate 193

plate 194

121

plate 195

plate 196

122

plate 197

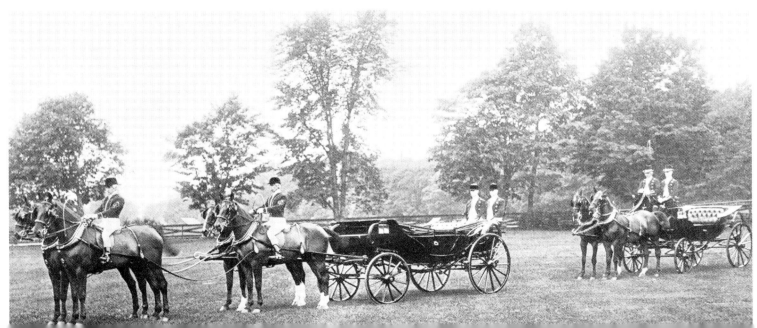

plate 198

123

plate 199

plate 201

plate 200

plate 202

touch was the presence of Prince George (Plate 196) for one splendid week. 'The Prince of Wales has taught the people of Quebec how to cheer,' was one of Grey's glowing reports to Edward VII.[126]

One of his proposals, the most ambitious of all, failed to materialize. It was for a colossal statue,[127] six inches higher than the Statue of Liberty in New York, towering above the cliff at Quebec and 'offering her welcoming outstretched arms to clasp the whole of the old world to her bosom.'[128] It was, as he reported to Buckingham Palace,

to have a lift inside to take visitors to the head, to look out through telescopes. In the chamber of the bosom below there will be kept a register of the subscribers —every child in the Empire will be able by the payment of 1/— or 6d. to write his or her name on the Heart of the Quebec Angel of Peace.[129]

When, however, he approached the royal children for their shillings he evidently encountered the disapproval of the Princess of Wales.

In 1909 the first competitions for his music and drama trophies were held. At the same time he was urging Canadian cities to build concert halls[130]—for which they have had to wait another sixty years. Equally foresightedly he advocated juvenile courts and commission government for cities.[131]

His combined Imperial and Canadian enthusiasms ran high that year. At a Press dinner at Rideau Hall he sounded the clarion call for Unity and made mention of Germany as Britian's rival.[132] After a Dominion Day dinner in London he wrote of his desire that Government House should be 'a Hive *always* filled with Imperial Bees.'[133] Later in July something he said on his trip to the Yukon was taken to be a description of that territory as 'a bower of roses and tulips,' and this raised great laughter in the press.[134]

In October he laid the corner-stones of the Parliament buildings at Regina (Plate 197) and Edmonton, reporting with satisfaction that in neither place did he see the Stars and Stripes flying.[135] He had banners, in *Art Nouveau* style, of St George and the Dragon made for distribution to Canadian schools.[136] These were probably inspired by Elgar's patriotic ballad of 1897, *The Banner of St George*, a current favourite with choral societies. In the meantime the government had opened an Office of External Affairs in Ottawa, on Grey's understanding that it would not interfere with his conduct of Imperial and foreign affairs.[137]

Nineteen-ten was to have been his last year in Canada. But Edward VII died in May—the memorial service this time being held on Parlia-

ment Hill[138]—and King George V informed him that the Duke of Connaught could not arrive at once as his successor. And so Grey agreed to stay another year.[139]

Turning his attention to the capital, he invited landscape designers[140] to consult on its improvement and had the satisfaction of seeing the first Ottawa driveway begun, the much criticized Lady Grey Drive along the Ottawa.[141] In order to strengthen his case for the building of a new Government House in Rockcliffe Park above the river—'the whole Empire does not contain a more noble site'—he held out the inducement of its becoming a royal palace before the end of the century.[142]

There were more travels. Perhaps it was on his trip to the United States in 1907, to meet President Taft, or on one of his visits to England, that Sargent drew a sensitive portrait of him[143] (Plate 205). In July he commenced the very long journey from Winnipeg through Hudson Bay (which incorrigibly he dubbed 'the Mediterranean of Canada')[144] to Newfoundland and eventually to Prince Edward Island. Feeling 'seedy' on his return in September—it was no wonder after all this—he also confessed to being downhearted at the slow progress of Imperial feeling in Canada.[145]

In January 1911 the Greys began their last months in Canada. It was decided to smarten up Rideau Hall for the arrival of royalty. Its state before alterations is recorded in an article in an American magazine, the author describing it extravagantly as rising 'like a great old-world castle, above its luxuriantly wooded surroundings.'[146] One of the illustrations is of Grey's state carriage (Plate 198), which he had bought from Lord Hopetoun who had used it in Australia, and which Grey sold to the government when he left.[147] Inside the house, the ballroom (Plate 199) with its deep ivory walls and gold damask curtains was hung with the St George banners and a caribou-skin banner presented by the Arctic Brotherhood. Lady Grey's sitting-room (Plates 200, 201) was bright with chintzes. From other sources we know that a 'cosy corner,' so typical of the decoration of the period, had been set up in the billiard room.[148] This and the greenhouses (Plate 202) were favourite sitting-out places for guests and are said to have been regularly inspected by the Governor-General during parties.

The chapel was still there, but new plans for the improvement of Rideau Hall called for its early removal[149] to make way for a cloak-room on the north side of the house. This in turn was to allow the more

plate 203

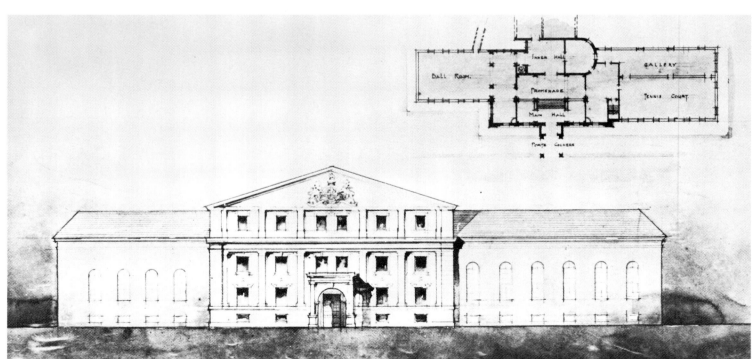

plate 204

126

ambitious project of a new main front to be carried out, of replacing the 'ignoble'[150] *porte-cochère* of the Monck period (Plate 203). The new façade was not built until the Connaught period (Plate 204).

The Duke of Connaught arrived in Canada late in the summer of 1911. The Borden government came into power shortly afterwards, and Canada entered an era which saw the attainment of her maturity through the fiery ordeal of the First World War.

Meanwhile the Greys had made their farewells. In a final address to the Canadian Club of Ottawa the Governor-General reviewed his period. If he had been too ardent an Imperialist he was unrepentant, and Anglo-Saxon civilization had been advanced. Canada, he declared, was growing up. When he arrived in 1904 she was still wearing colonial dress, but the garrisons at Halifax and Esquimalt had since been withdrawn and she now contributed to her own defence. Soon she would be admitted to the councils of the Empire.[151]

Grey's last few years were unspectacular. Before his death in England in 1917 he unveiled the Cecil Rhodes monument in South Africa and became president of the Royal Colonial Institute (now the Royal Commonwealth Society) in London. He did not live long enough to see, as we do today, so many of his remarkable prophecies concerning Canada being fulfilled (Plate 205).

plate 205

REFERENCES

INTRODUCTION

1. By a correspondent of the *Philadelphia Quiz*, in W. Stewart MacNutt, *Days of Lorne* (Fredericton, 1955) [MacNutt], p. 201.

I

BEGINNINGS

1. See Robert Legget, *Rideau Waterway* (Toronto, 1955), pp. 21 ff.
2. *The Canadian Portrait Gallery* (Toronto, 1881), vol. 4, pp. 134-137; F. J. Audet, 'Thomas McKay, Rideau Hall, and Earnscliffe,' C.H.A. *Report*, 1932, pp. 65-79; Wilfrid Eggleston, *The Queen's Choice* (Ottawa, 1961), pp. 26, 91-92; Legget, *Rideau Waterway*, p. 195.
3. 'Additions and Improvements to Rideau Hall,' dated 13 June 1865, in Appendix 14, D.P.W. Rep., 1866; see also D.P.W. Rec., Description of Rideau Hall by F. J. Rubidge, dated 4 April 1864.
4. *The Canada Directory*, 2 vol. (Montreal, 1857), vol. 1, p. 464.
5. Letter, dated 15 June 1853, in *International Journal*, quoted in Audet, 'Thomas McKay, Rideau Hall, and Earnscliffe,' p.76.
6. *Free Press*, Ottawa, 21 Oct. 1878.
7. Dorothy Stroud, *The Architecture of Sir John Soane* (London, 1961).
8. Letter to writer, 7 Dec. 1963.
9. Stroud, *The Architecture of Sir John Soane*, pp. 31, 35, Pls. 9, 10, 53.
10. Marion McRae and Anthony Adamson, *The Ancestral Roof* (Toronto, 1963), pp. 112-113.
11. *Ibid.*, pp. 102-106.
12. Audet, 'Thomas McKay, Rideau Hall, and Earnscliffe,' p. 76.
13. *Ibid.*
14. D.P.W. Rec., Description of Rideau Hall by F. J. Rubidge, dated 4 April 1864.
15. *Ottawa Journal*, Coronation ed., 2 June 1953.
16. Eggleston, *The Queen's Choice*, p. 108.
17. Robert Cellem, *The Visit of His Royal Highness The Prince of Wales to the British North American Provinces* (Toronto, 1861), p. 192.
18. Quoted in Eggleston, *The Queen's Choice*, p. 131.
19. Report, Commissioners of Public Works, 1862; Alan H. Armstrong, 'Profile of Parliament Hill,' *Royal Architectural Institute of Canada Journal*, vol. 34 (1957), pp. 327-331.
20. For subsequent additions and alterations and for expenditures, see D.P.W. Rep., 1867-1905; see also D.P.W. Rec., 1864-1867.
21. For Monck's earlier years in Canada see J. A. Gibson, 'The Duke of Newcastle and British North American Affairs' *C.H.R.*, vol. 44 (1963), pp, 142-156. For the life of Lord Monck, see *D.N.B.*, Supplement vol. 3, pp. 183-184.
22. C. P. Stacey, 'Lord Monck and the Canadian Nation,' *Dalhousie Review*, vol. 14 (1934-5), pp. 179-191.
23. P.A.C., Monck Papers.
24. Frances Monck, *My Canadian Leaves* (London, 1891).
25. Destroyed by fire, February 1966.
26. Frances Monck, *My Canadian Leaves*, p. 152.
27. *Ibid.*, p. 154.
28. *Ibid.*, p. 174.
29. *Ibid.*, p. 152.
30. See C. C. J. Bond, 'The Canadian Government Comes to Ottawa,' *Ontario History*, vol. 55 (1963), pp. 23-34.
31. In Sir Joseph Pope, *Memoirs of the Right Honourable Sir John Alexander Macdonald* (Ottawa, 1894) vol. 1, pp. 266-267.
32. 'Additions and Improvements to Rideau Hall,' *op. cit.*
33. See D.P.W. Rec., Specifications by F. J. Rubidge, dated 8 May 1865.
34. See D.P.W. Rec., Estimates, Oct. 1886-May 1867.
35. Monck Papers, Monck to Henry Monck, 3 May 1866.
36. Ottawa *Citizen*, 3 May 1866.
37. See D.P.W. Rec., Specifications, Oct. 1866.
38. General Report, Minister of Public Works, 1867-82.
39. Monck Papers, Monck to Henry Monck, 26 June 1867.
40. Creighton I, p. 476.
41. Creighton II, pp. 1-2.
42. Monck Papers, Monck to Henry Monck, 16 Feb. 1867.
43. *Ibid.*, 17 May 1866.
44. *Ibid.*, 27 Oct. 1867.
45. *Ibid.*, 31 May 1866.
46. *Ibid.*, 10 May 1867.
47. Meredith, 26 March 1868.
48. *Ibid.*, 10 Sept. 1867.
49. *Ibid.*, 13 and 27 June 1866; 7 March 1866.
50. Monck Papers, Monck to Henry Monck, 28 June 1866.
51. *Ibid.*, 22 Nov. 1867.
52. Meredith, 13 June 1866.
53. Bond, 'The Canadian Government Comes to Ottawa,' p. 33; Meredith, 1 Aug. 1866.
54. Meredith, 13 June 1866.
55. *Ottawa Journal*, Coronation ed., 2 June 1953.
56. Macdonald to Tupper, 25 May 1868, in Stacey, 'Lord Monck and the Canadian Nation,' p. 189; Meredith, 5 May 1868.
57. In Creighton I, p. 479.
58. General Report, Minister of Public Works, 1867-82, pp. xxi, 180.
59. *Ibid.*, p. 180.
60. *D.N.B.*, vol. 72, p. 382; Pope, *Macdonald*, vol. 2, pp. 15-17.
61. Young arrived in Ottawa at the earliest on the evening of the 27 Nov. 1868 and at the latest the next morning, not in December 1868 or in 1869 as in some accounts (see *Citizen*, Ottawa, 4 Dec. 1868, for his arrival at Prescott, Ontario, on 27 Nov.).
62. Speech, Montreal, 20 June 1872, in *Speeches of the Earl of Dufferin* (Toronto 1878), p. 9.
63. P.A.C. (microfilm), Kimberley Papers, Lisgar to Kimberley, 8 Aug. 1870.
64. *Ibid.*, 20 April 1871; 4 May 1871.
65. *Ottawa Journal,* Coronation ed., 2 June 1953.
66. P.A.C. Lisgar Papers, newspaper cutting, 1 Jan. 1869.
67. *Ottawa Journal*, Coronation ed., 2 June 1953.
68. Meredith, 10 June 1869.

69. Florence Hamilton Randal, 'Rideau Hall—Past and Present,' *Canadian Magazine*, vol. 12 (1898) [Randal], p. 151.
70. Mary Howard McClintock, *The Queen Thanks Sir Howard* (London, 1945), Chap. 20.
71. *Ibid.*, p. 118.
72. *Ibid.*, p. 131.
73. D.P.W. Rep., 1867-1882, Entries for 1869.
74. Kimberley Papers, Lisgar to Kimberley, 2 Sept. 1870.
75. *Ibid.*, Lisgar to Kimberley, 16 and 26 Oct. 1871.
76. Speech, Montreal, 20 June 1872, in *Speeches of the Earl of Dufferin*, p. 10.

II

THE SEVENTIES

1. For hearsay that Dufferin was the natural son of Disraeli, see D. M. L. Farr, 'Lord Dufferin, A Viceroy in Ottawa,' *Culture*, vol. 19 (1958), pp. 153-4.
2. George Stewart, *Canada under the Administration of the Earl of Dufferin* (Toronto, 1878); William Leggo, *History of the Administration of the Right Hon. Frederick Temple, Earl of Dufferin* (Montreal, 1878) [Leggo]; *D.N.B.*, 2nd Suppl., vol. 1, pp. 171-176; C.E.D. Black, *The Marquess of Dufferin and Ava* (Toronto, 1903); Sir Alfred Lyall, *The Life of the Marquis of Dufferin and Ava* (2 vol., Toronto, 1905) [Lyall]; Harold Nicholson, *Helen's Tower* (London, 1937); C. W. de Kiewiet and F. H. Underhill, eds., *The Dufferin-Carnarvon Correspondence, 1874-1878* (Toronto, Champlain Society, 1955) [D.-C. Corr.]; D. M. L. Farr, 'Lord Dufferin, a Viceroy in Ottawa,' *Culture*, xix (1958), pp. 153-164.
3. Nicholson, *Helen's Tower*, p. 42.
4. Lord Dufferin, *Letters from High Latitudes* (London, 1860).
5. Nicholson, *Helen's Tower*, pp. 134, 143 ff.
6. In *D.-C. Corr.*, Introduction, pp. xi-xii.
7. Lady Dufferin, *My Canadian Journal* (New York, 1891) [*Journal*].
8. *Speeches of the Earl of Dufferin* [*Speeches*].
9. See Dufferin to Lady Dartrey, 24 July 1872, in Lyall, vol. 1, p. 204.
10. Macdonald to Lisgar, 2 Sept. 1872, in Sir Joseph Pope, ed., *Correspondence of Sir John Macdonald* (Toronto, 1921), p. 177; see also Meredith, 18 Dec. 1872.
11. In Lyall, vol. 1, p. 215.
12. Dufferin to Lady Dartrey, 5 Sept. 1872, in Lyall, vol. 1, p. 213.
13. MacNutt, pp. 16-17.
14. Meredith, 18 Dec. 1872.
15. In MacNutt, p. 17; see also Kimberley Papers, Dufferin to Kimberley, 31 Oct. 1872.
16. *Journal*, 27 June 1872.
17. *Ibid.*, 28 June 1872.
18. *Ibid.* 1 July 1872.
19. For these and other items, see D.P.W. Rec., 1872-3.
20. Lieutenant-Colonel Henry Charles Fletcher (d. 1879), secretary to Lord Dufferin, 1872-5.
21. D. P. W. Rec., Fletcher to Minister of Public Works, 29 June 1872.
22. For plans by Thomas Seaton Scott, 31 July 1872, see D. P. W. Rec., 1872.
23. *Journal*, 27 July 1872.
24. Kimberley Papers, Dufferin to Kimberley, 30 July 1872.
25. *Ibid.*, Dufferin to Kimberley, 12 Aug. 1872; see also Dufferin to Lady Dartrey, 24 July 1872, in Lyall, vol. 1, pp. 212-213.
26. *Journal*, Chap. 2. Dufferin wrote, on taking possession of the Governor-General's quarters after completion of the alterations: 'I have at least succeeded in fighting my way into the citadel of Quebec, though Wolfe scarcely met with greater difficulties in doing so,' in Lyall, vol. 1, p. 213.

27. John E. Parsons, *West on the 49th Parallel* (New York, 1963), p. 29.
28. *Ibid.*
29. *Journal*, Chap. 3.
30. *Ibid.*, 2 Nov. 1872.
31. Randal, pp. 152-154; *Journal*, 25 Dec. 1872.
32. *Journal*, 27 Nov. 1872.
33. D. P. W. Rec., Memorandum, 20 Jan. 1873.
34. *Ibid.*, 10 June, 3 July, 5 Nov. 1872.
35. *Journal*, 3 Dec. 1872.
36. Stewart, *Administration of the Earl of Dufferin*, p. 143.
37. Randal, p. 155.
38. Meredith, 18 Dec. 1872, 18 Dec. 1877.
39. *Journal*, 28 Dec. 1872.
40. *D.-C. Corr.*, Dufferin to Carnarvon, 9 March 1876.
41. Kimberley Papers, Dufferin to Kimberley, 16 Jan. 1873; see also *D.-C. Corr.*, Memorandum, Dufferin to Carnarvon, 24 July 1875 (pp. 153-154).
42. Kimberley Papers, Dufferin to Kimberley, 19 Feb. 1873; see also Dufferin to Duke of Argyll, in Lyall, vol. 1, pp. 216-217.
43. D.P.W. Rec., William Hutchison to Braun, 3 July 1874. Dufferin contributed $1,624.95 towards the skating and curling rinks and the toboggan slide in 1872-3.
44. D.P.W. Rec., 5 Oct. 1872 ff.; *Journal*, 4 March 1873 ff.
45. D.P.W. Rec., Memorandum, Feb. 1875.
46. *Journal*, 13 March 1873.
47. *To Oblige Benson* was an 1854 comedy of married life by the Tom Taylor of Lord Dundreary fame. Also played during the season was *The First Night* (probably the farce by J. M. Maddox).
48. *Journal*, 15 April 1873; D.P.W. Rec., 12 Nov. 1873.
49. *Journal*, 22 June 1873.
50. Kimberley Papers, Dufferin to Kimberley, 23 July 1873.
51. *Ibid.*, Dufferin to Kimberley, 5 Aug. 1873; Lyall, vol. 1, p. 221.
52. Kimberley Papers, Dufferin to Kimberley, 5 Aug. 1873.
53. *Journal*, 17 Oct. 1873.
54. D.P.W. Rec., Memorandum, 15 Sept. 1873.
55. *Journal*, 1 Jan. 1874.
56. *Ibid.*, 6 March 1874.
57. *Ibid.*, 28 Feb. 1874.
58. *Ibid.*, 2 April 1874.
59. *Ibid.*, 7 April 1874.
60. *Ibid.*, 25 May 1874.
61. Speech, 27 July 1874, in *Speeches*, p. 51.
62. *Journal*, 17 Aug. 1874.
63. Leggo, p. 268.
64. Speech, Brockville, 7 Sept. 1874, in *Speeches*, p. 64. For the tour as a whole, see Dufferin to Duchess of Argyll, 28 Sept. and 9 Oct. 1874, in Lyall, vol. 1, pp. 238-247.
65. Dufferin to Duchess of Argyll, 18 Nov. 1874, in Lyall, vol. 1, pp. 151-256; *Journal*, 23 Oct. 1874 ff.
66. Albert Bierstadt (1830-1902) was born at Solingen, Germany, and was brought to the United States in infancy. He studied in Düsseldorf and Rome and made his first trip to the American west in 1858. He became known for his western landscapes. He lived in New York and Irvington-on-Hudson and died in New York.
67. *Journal*, 31 Oct. 1874.
68. *Ibid.*, 28 Nov. 1874.
69. *Ibid.*, 15 Dec. 1874.
70. Parsons, *West on the 49th Parallel*, pp. 130-131.

71. Two other plays were performed in March 1875: *A Happy Pair* by S. Theyre Smith and *School* by Tom Robertson.
72. *Journal*, 31 March 1875.
73. *Ibid.*, 26 Oct. 1874. Lieutenant-Colonel The Hon. Edward George Percy Littleton (1842-1930) was secretary to Lord Dufferin, 1875-8, and to Lord Lorne, 1878-9. He succeeded to the peerage in 1888 as 3rd Baron Hatherton.
74. *D.-C. Corr.*, Dufferin to Carnarvon, 23 Dec. 1875.
75. *Journal*, 22 March 1876.
76. An oil painting of tobogganing, probably at Rideau Hall, was sold at Parke-Bernet, New York, in 1965 (Plate 49).
77. *Journal*, 3 Nov. 1875 ff., 10 March 1876; see also D.P.W. Rec., Memorandum, 9 Feb. 1876, concerning an account for a 'Decorative Tent' imported from New York at $668.28.
78. *Journal*, 11 March 1876.
79. *Ibid.*, 22 March 1876; Leggo, pp. 426-429.
80. D.P.W. Rec., Memorandum, 30 April 1875.
81. *Ibid.*, Plans submitted by J. W. H. Watts, 25 Feb. 1875; see also Memorandum, 30 March 1876. The building is now used as a summer barrack for guards at Rideau Hall.
82. *Journal*, Chaps, 15, 16.
83. *Ibid.*, 25-29 July 1876.
84. *Ibid.*, 1 Aug. 1876.
85. Leggo, pp. 455-473; Lyall, vol. 1, pp. 272-274.
86. Black, *The Marquess of Dufferin*, p. 133; Speech, Ottawa, 23 Oct. 1876, in *Speeches*, pp. 86-87. The Canadian section of the Philadelphia Centennial Exposition included displays of minerals, manufactures, etc.; the art section included contributions from Jean-Baptiste Côté (a ship's figure-head), Notman (photographs), and Forshaw Day (paintings).
87. Speech, Ottawa, 23 Oct. 1876, in *Speeches*, pp. 86-87.
88. *D.-C. Corr.*, Dufferin to Carnarvon, 20 and 23 Nov. 1876.
89. Stewart, *Administration of the Earl of Dufferin*, p. 28.
90. *D.-C. Corr.*, 20 Nov. 1876.
91. *Ibid.*, Dufferin to Carnarvon, 18 March 1874.
92. *Ibid.*
93. *Ibid.*
94. Dufferin to Lady Dorothy Nevill, Dec. 1875, in Lyall, pp. 266-267.
95. Speech, 13 Jan., 1877, in *Speeches*, p. 90.
96. Speech, 12 Jan. 1877, in *Speeches*, p. 88.
97. Lyall, p. 251.
98. *Journal*, 30 April 1877.
98a. *Ibid.*, 7 May 1877.
99. *D.-C. Corr.*, Dufferin to Carnarvon, 9 Oct. 1877.
100. *Journal*. 2 Oct. 1877. This was on the return journey, in the United States.
101. *D.-C. Corr.*, Dufferin to Carnarvon, 1 Nov. 1877.
102. *Ibid.*, Carnarvon to Dufferin, 25 April 1877.
103. Speech, 15 Feb. 1878, in *Speeches*, p. 105; Meredith, 12 April 1878; *Journal*, 15 Feb. 1878. The picture was recently sold by the Montreal Museum of Fine Arts.
104. Speech, 21 May 1878, in *Speeches*, p. 106.
105. *Journal*, 2 and 5 April 1878.
106. *Ibid.*, 2 April 1878; Black, *Marquess of Dufferin*, p. 154.
107. *Journal*, 17 May 1878.
108. Meredith, 16 April 1878.
109. *Ibid.*, 16 April 1878; Leggo, pp. 729-730; *Journal*, 16 April 1878.
110. *Journal*, 30 April and 3 May 1878.
111. Meredith, 11 May 1878; Leggo, pp. 731-732.
112. *Journal*, 17 May 1878.
113. *Ibid.*, 6 June 1878.
114. Speech, 7 June 1878, in *Speeches*, p. 110.
115. *Journal*, 7 June 1878.
116. *Ibid.*, 30 Aug. 1878; Dufferin since 1875 had worked for the preservation of the walls and gates of Quebec; see *D.-C. Corr.*, Dufferin to Carnarvon, 2 Dec. 1875; Lyall, vol. 1, pp. 263-264.
117. *Journal*, 31 Aug. 1878.
118. Nicholson, *Helen's Tower*, pp. 265-276; Lyall, vol. 2, pp. 304-305.

III

THE EIGHTIES

1. The examples in Plate 60 (in the writer's collection) bear a stamp which, according to Mr Gerald Stevens of the Royal Ontario Museum, indicates manufacture in England.
2. Creighton II, p. 248.
3. MacNutt, pp. 201-202.
4. Creighton II, p. 255; see also pp. 248-255.
5. Duke of Argyll (Marquess of Lorne), *Passages from the Past* (2 vol., London, 1907) [*Passages*], vol. 2, p. 410; P.A.C., Lorne Papers, Government House Diary and Engagement Book [*Diary*], 25 and 26 Nov. 1878; MacNutt, pp. 10-11.
6. Diary, 29 Nov. and 1 Dec. 1878.
7. Creighton II, p. 248.
8. MacNutt, p. 8.
9. Marquess of Lorne, *Canadian Pictures* (London, 1884); Lorne, *Memories of Canada and Scotland* (Montreal, 1884) [*Memories*]; D.N.B., 1912-1921, pp. 87-88; Frances Lady Balfour, *Ne Obliviscaris* (2 vol., London, 1930) [*Balfour*]; MacNutt.
10. Queen Victoria, *Leaves from the Journal of Our Life in the Highlands* (New York, 1868), p. 89.
11. Balfour, vol. 1, p. 82.
12. *Ibid.*, vol. 1, pp. 87, 98, 110.
13. In his *Book of Psalms, Literally Rendered into Verse* (1877).
14. Lorne, *A Trip to the Tropics* (London, 1867), pp. 344-355; see also MacNutt, pp. 5-7.
14a. *D.N.B.*, 1931-1949, pp. 544-545.
15. MacNutt, p. 9.
16. Balfour, vol. 1, p. 103.
17. In *Passages*, vol. 2, p. 396.
18. Dated Osborne, 20 July 1878, in G. E. Buckle, ed., *The Letters of Queen Victoria*, vol. 2 (Toronto, 1926), pp. 630-631.
19. Meredith, 2 Dec. 1878; Diary, 2 Dec. 1878; MacNutt, p. 15.
20. General Selbye Smith, in Militia Report, 1878. This troop, formerly called the Ottawa Troop of Cavalry, was redesignated the Princess Louise Dragoon Guards in 1879.
21. D.P.W. Rec., Register, Rideau Hall, 1879-1896, Entry for 18 Feb. 1880.
22. *Ibid.*, 6 Aug. 1878.
23. D.P.W. Rep., 1878-9; 1879-80.
24. Diary, 8 Jan. 1879.
25. Lorne to Duke of Argyll, 4 Dec. 1878, in MacNutt, p. 242.
26. *Ibid.*, p. 244.
27. G. M. Grant, *Picturesque Canada* (2 vol., Toronto, 1882 ff.), vol. 1, p. 187.
28. For an extensive account of social events, see J. E. Collins, *Canada under the Administration of Lord Lorne* (Toronto, 1884), Chap. 8; see also Grant, *Picturesque Canada*, vol. 1, pp. 189-192; MacNutt, pp. 206-207.
29. MacNutt, pp. 201-203.

30. *Ibid.*, pp. 127-128; *Passages*, vol. 2, pp. 412-413, 417. Dr Eugene Forsey, in a paper, 'Meetings of the Queen's Privy Council for Canada, 1867-1882' (1966), points out that Dufferin presided only over formal Privy Council meetings and not those of Cabinet.
31. MacNutt, Chap. 2.
32. Lorne to Duke of Argyll, 4 Dec. 1878, in MacNutt, p. 244; see also D.N.B., 2nd Suppl., vol. 1, p. 494. Francis (later Sir Francis) de Winton (1835-1901) was A.D.C. and later secretary to Sir Fenwick Williams in Nova Scotia before serving as secretary to Lord Lorne, 1878-1883; after his period in Canada he became an administrator in South Africa.
33. Lady Byng of Vimy, *Up the Stream of Time* (Toronto, 1945), pp. 11-12.
34. Personal recollection, 1963.
35. Dated Osborne, 1 Jan. 1879, in G. E. Buckle, ed., *The Letters of Queen Victoria*, vol. 3 (London, 1928), p. 4.
36. Entries in the four volumes of the Diary cover the period from 13 Nov. 1878 to 28 Feb. 1883.
37. Creighton II, p. 258.
38. Diary, 26 March 1879.
39. Lorne to Duke of Argyll, 30 April 1879, in MacNutt, p. 246.
40. National Gallery of Canada (Accession No. 144).
41. *Passages*, vol. 2, pp. 417-419; Diary, 6 Jan. 1879.
42. The plays performed between 1879 and 1881 included *Alone; Woodcock's Little Game; Used up; Cool as a Cucumber; Perfection:* and *Betsy Baker;* see MacNutt, pp. 207-208.
43. Annie Howells Fréchette, 'Life at Rideau Hall,' *Harper's New Monthly Magazine*, vol. 63 (1881), pp. 213-223.
44. *Ibid*,. p. 214.
45. Cf. D.P.W. Rec., Register, Rideau Hall, Entries for Feb. 1880 and March 1883.
46. Fréchette, 'Life at Rideau Hall,' p. 217.
47. *Ibid.*, p. 222.
48. I am here incorporating some of the material in 'A Day with the Marquis of Lorne at Rideau Hall, Ottawa,' *Frank Leslies' Illustrated Newspaper*, vol. 49 (7 Feb. 1880), pp. 422-423.
49. Fréchette, 'Life at Rideau Hall,' p. 222.
50. Door of the room now used as an office of the lady-in-waiting.
51. D.P.W. Rec., Richard Moreton to Chief Architect, 9 July 1879.
52, 'A Day with the Marquis of Lorne,' p. 423.
53. *Memories*, pp. 214-220.
54. Diary, 14 Nov. 1879.
55. *Ibid.*, 9 June 1879.
56. *Ibid.*, 11 June 1879. The Cantata of Welcome to words by Napoléon Legendre, culminated in a simultaneous rendition of 'God Save The Queen,' 'Vive la canadienne,' and 'Comin' through the Rye' (Kallman, *History of Music in Canada*, Toronto, 1960).
57. Balfour, vol. 1, pp. 297-298.
58. Four volumes of Princess Louise's water colours, many of Canadian subjects, are in the National Gallery of Canada (Accession Nos. 14638, 14641, 14643, 14657).
59. Diary, 8 Sept. 1879.
60. MacNutt, p. 214.
61. *Ibid.*, p. 215.
62. Quoted in *D.N.B.*, 1912-1921, p. 87; see also Creighton II, p. 279.
63. See Note 48, Chap. III, also Diary, 17 Jan. 1880.
64. 'A Day with the Marquis of Lorne,' p. 422.
65. *Ibid.*, p. 423.
65a. *Ibid.*
66. Diary, 11 Feb. 1880.

66a. Lt (later Lt-Col.) William Bagot (1857-1932) succeeded as 4th Baron Bagot in 1887.
67. *Ibid.*, 14 Feb. 1880.
68. *Passages*, vol. 2, p. 444.
69. Balfour, vol. 1, pp. 320-321.
70. MacNutt, p. 217.
71. *Ibid.*, p. 206.
72. See Macdonald to Lorne, 26 Jan. 1881, in MacNutt, pp. 171-172.
73. MacNutt, p. 220.
74. Diary, 24 and 28 Feb. 1880.
75. C. C. J. Bond, 'The True North,' *Queen's Quarterly*, vol. 69 (1962), pp. 391-394; *Memories*, pp. 14-16 (a different version of seven stanzas and refrain); Duke of Argyll (Marquess of Lorne), *Yesterday & To-day in Canada* (London, 1910), p. xvi; MacNutt, pp. 207-208.
76. MacNutt, Chap. 8.
77. *Passages*, vol. 2, p. 444; *Memories*, pp. 251-256; MacNutt, p. 137; R. H. Hubbard, 'The Early Years of the National Gallery of Canada,' *Transactions, Royal Society of Canada*, vol. 3, ser. 4 (1965), pp. 121-129.
78. Albert Bierstadt (see note 66, Chap. II) was a frequent visitor to Rideau Hall and the Citadel during the Lorne period and must have had a considerable influence on L. R. O'Brien.
79. Now, after alterations, used for government offices; see P.A.C., Macdonald Papers, Macdonald to Lorne [Dec. 1879 or Jan. 1880].
80. *Passages*, vol. 2, p. 447.
81. For quotations from Ottawa newspapers, see Hubbard, 'The Early Years of the National Gallery of Canada,' p. 122.
82. *Memories*, pp. 251-252.
83. Diary, 3 June 1880.
84. Bond, 'The True North,' pp. 393-394; Kimberley Papers, Lorne to Kimberley, 1 July 1880.
85. Cf. MacNutt, pp. 218-220.
86. 'Captain Mac' (J. T. McAdam), *Canada; from the Lakes to the Gulf* (Montreal, 1881).
87. *Ibid.*, pp. 47-49.
88. Kimberley Papers, Lorne to Kimberley, 12 Sept. 1880.
89. Creighton II, p. 310.
90. The Rev. James ('Hamish') McGregor (1832-1910), minister of St Cuthbert's, Edinburgh, was moderator of the Church of Scotland in 1891; he travelled widely and published accounts of his travels in *The Scotsman*.
91. *Passages*, vol. 2, p. 462.
92. Kimberley Papers, Lorne to Kimberley, 3 May 1881.
93. *Passages*, vol. 2, p. 459.
94. *Picturesque Canada* (see note 27, Chap. III) had been issued periodically prior to publication in book form.
95. *Passages*, vol. 2, p. 463.
96. Lorne, *Yesterday & To-day in Canada*, pp. 97-101. For an amusing anecdote of the powwow, see Sir Joseph Pope, *The Tour of Their Royal Highnesses, The Duke and Duchess of Cornwall and York through the Dominion of Canada in the Year 1901* (Ottawa, 1903), pp. 79-80.
97. Balfour, vol. 1, p. 328.
98. *Passages*, vol. 2, p. 460.
99. *Ibid.*
100. Creighton II, pp. 337, 354.
101. Hubbard, 'The Early Years of the National Gallery of Canada,' p. 123.
102. Kimberley Papers, Kimberley to Lorne, 25 May 1882.
103. MacNutt, pp. 171-172.

104. *Ibid.*, p. 212.
105. Diary, 22 and 27 June 1882.
106. Macdonald Papers, Macdonald to Lorne, 12 Aug. 1882. For the trip see *Passages*, vol. 2, pp. 475-492.
107. For financial accounts for the western tour, see P.A.C., Lorne Papers, 1882-3.
108. E. S. G. Heyl, *Bermuda through the Camera of James B. Heyl* (Hamilton, 1951), pp. 191-204; Terry Tucker, 'Fourteen Royal Visits to Bermuda', *Bermuda Historical Quarterly*, vol. 10 (1953), pp. 153-158; Sister J. de Chantal Kennedy, *Biography of a Colonial Town* (Hamilton, 1961), pp. 337-338.
109. *Passages*, vol. 2, p. 491.
110. Lorne of Duke of Argyll, 2 March 1883, in MacNutt, p. 257.
111. *Passages*, vol. 2, p. 495.
112. *Memories*, pp. 330-335.
113. *Ibid.*, pp. 343-344; Harold Nicholson, *King George The Fifth* (London, 1952), p. 35.
114. *Memories, p.* 349.
115. *Passages*, vol. 2, p. 497.
116. *Memories*, pp. 352-353.
117. Macdonald Papers, Macdonald to Lorne, 11 July 1883.
118. Balfour, vol. 2, p. 381.
119. Lorne, *Yesterday & To-day in Canada*, Chap. xv.
120. Creighton II, p. 354.
121. Macdonald Papers, Macdonald to Lorne, 9 and 27 June 1883; Creighton II, p. 37.
122. Lord Newton, *Lord Lansdowne, a Biography* (London, 1929) [Newton]; *D.N.B.*, 1922-1930, pp. 667-675.
123. Prince Leopold, Duke of Albany, had been proposed as governor-general. For Lord Derby's recommendation of Lansdowne in his place, see P.A.C. (microfilm), Derby Papers, Derby to Queen Victoria, 8 and 17 May 1883; also Sir Henry Ponsonby to Derby, in G. E. Buckle, ed., *The Letters of Queen Victoria*, 2nd ser., vol. 3 (London, 1928), p. 422. Prince Leopold, who suffered from haemophilia, died in 1884.
124. Lady Maud Hamilton, duaghter of the Duke of Abercorn.
125. Creighton II, pp. 355-356; Newton, p. 26.
126. Macdonald to Lorne, 26 Oct. 1883, in Creighton II, p. 356.
127. John Buchan, *Lord Minto, a Memoir* (London, 1924), Chap. 4; Lady Minto, in Countess of Oxford and Asquith, ed., *Myself when Young by Famous Women of To-day* (London, 1938) [*Myself when Young*], p. 229.
128. Newton, pp. 27-28.
129. Lansdowne to his mother, 15 July 1884, in Newton, p. 30.
130. Derby Papers, Lansdowne to Derby, 30 May 1884.
131. The house, on the Cascapedia River, was named New Derreen after the Lansdowne house in Kerry; see Newton, p. 29.
132. Lord Frederic Hamilton, 'The Days Before Yesterday' in *My Yesterdays* (New York, 1921).
133. *Ibid.*, p. 255.
134. *Ibid.*, pp. 259-261.
135. *Ibid.*, p. 261.
136. *Ibid.*, pp. 262-3.
137. *Ibid.*, pp. 267-269.
138. *Ibid.*, p. 270.
139. *Ibid.*, p. 275.
140. *Ibid.*, p. 284.
141. P.A.C., Lansdowne Papers, Government House Account Books, 1886-8.
142. Lansdowne to his mother, 26 March 1885, in Newton, p. 32.
143. *Ibid.*, 1 Oct. 1885, in Newton, p. 37.

144. *Ibid.*, 11 Oct. 1885, in Newton, p. 40.
145. Newton, p. 42.
146. George T. Denison, *Soldiering in Canada* (Toronto, 1901), p. 343.
147. Newton, p. 45 (Queen Victoria to Lansdowne, 3 June 1887).
148. During the Lansdowne period the inclusion of Newfoundland and the West Indies in the Canadian Confederation was broached; see Lansdowne Papers, Lansdowne to Derby, 30 May and 3 July 1884 and 9 June 1885.
149. Lansdowne to Sir Henry Holland, 24 Nov. 1887, in Newton, p. 48.
150. Lansdowne to his mother, 1 Dec. 1887, in Newton, p. 49.
151. Newton, p. 53. In 1917 Lansdowne underwent severe criticism for the 'Lansdowne Letter,' in which he raised the question of peace before the destruction of Europe.
152. *D.N.B.*, 2nd Suppl., vol. 3, pp. 381-383.
153. Lady Isobel Gathorne-Hardy (1875-1964).
154. Lady Constance Villiers, daughter of the Earl of Clarendon.
155. Captain (later Lt-Col.) Josceline Bagot (1854-1913), Grenadier Guards, was A.D.C. to Lord Stanley 1888-9.
156. Personal recollection of Lady Isobel Gathorne-Hardy, 1962.
157. *Ibid.*
158. O. D. Skelton, *Sir Wilfrid Laurier* (2 vol., Toronto, 1921), p. 424.
159. E. A. Collard, *Gazette*, Montreal (21 July 1956).
160. At a concert on 15 Dec. 1891 Arthur and Heinrich Grünfeld, court pianist and cellist respectively to the emperors of Germany and Austria, played works by Beethoven, Wagner, Schumann, and Boccherini.
161. The plays performed included *Cut off with a Shilling* and *Dearest Mama*.
162. J. T. Saywell, ed., *The Canadian Journal of Lady Aberdeen, 1893-1898* (Toronto, Champlain Society, 1960), 12 Aug. 1896; Canada Council, *Bulletin*, No. 11 (1962), pp. 1-2.
163. Nicholson, *King George The Fifth*, p. 42.
164. P.A.C. (microfilm), Stanley Papers.
165. *Ibid.*, Stanley to Macdonald [May 1891].
166. Personal recollection of Lady Isobel Gathorne-Hardy.
167. Lady Aberdeen, *Through Canada with a Kodak* (Edinburgh, 1893), pp. 13-14, 76-78.
168. By Piranesi (recollection by Lady Isobel Gathorne-Hardy).
169. P.A.C., Aberdeen Papers, Lady Derby to Lady Aberdeen, 22 May 1893.

IV

THE NINETIES

1. Marjorie Lady Pentland, *A Bonnie Fechter: the Life of Ishbel Marjoribanks, Marchioness of Aberdeen and Temair* (London, 1952) [Pentland].
2. Lord and Lady Aberdeen, *More Cracks with "We Twa"* (London, 1929) [*More Cracks*], p. 95.
3. *More Cracks*, Chap. 8.
4. Lady Aberdeen, *Through Canada with a Kodak*. This book was originally written in the form of articles for her periodical for young people, *Onward and Upward*; the MS, illustrated with her photographs, is in Aberdeen Papers, P.A.C.
5. J. T. Saywell, ed., *The Canadian Journal of Lady Aberdeen, 1893-1898* (Toronto, Champlain Society, 1960) [Can. Journal], p. xxix; see also pp. xxiv, xxxii. The full MS is in Aberdeen Papers, P.A.C.
6. *Can. Journal*, pp. xiii ff., xxv; Pentland; Lord and Lady Aberdeen, *We Twa, Reminiscences of Lord and Lady Aberdeen* (2 vol., London, 1925) [*We Twa*]; *More Cracks*; Lady Aberdeen, *Musings of a Scottish Granny* (London, 1936) [*Musings*]; *D.N.B.*, 1931-1940, pp. 348-349.
7. *Can. Journal*, pp. xiv ff.; *D.N.B.*, 1931-1940, pp. 347-348.
8. *Ibid.*, pp. xviii-xix.

9. *We Twa*, vol. 2, Chap. 1.
10. *Musings*, Chap. 14.
11. *We Twa*, vol. 2, pp. 88-91.
12. *Ibid.*, vol. 1, p. 246.
13. For a full list see *Can. Journal*, pp. 504-506.
14. *Archie Gordon* [memorial volume] (Privately printed, 1910).
15. *We Twa*, vol. 2, pp. 51, 205; *More Cracks*, pp. 95-96; *Archie Gordon*, p. 3.
16. *Can. Journal*, 17 Sept. 1893; *We Twa*, vol. 2, pp. 13-15.
17. *Can Journal*, p. xxv.
18. *Ibid.*, 18 Sept. 1893.
19. *Ibid.*, 26 Sept. 1893.
20. See J. D. Edgar, *Canada and its Capital* (Toronto, 1898), Chap. 10.
21. *Can. Journal*, 27 and 28 Oct. 1893; *We Twa*, vol. 2, Chap 8.
22. *Canada Journal*, 12 Nov. 1893.
23. D.P.W. Rep., 1894; 1895; D.P.W. Rec., Registers, Rideau Hall, March-April 1894.
24. *We Twa*, vol. 2, p. 209; *More Cracks*, pp. 104-105.
25. *Can. Journal*, 20 Dec. 1893.
26. *Ibid.*, 24 Dec. 1893.
27. *We Twa*, vol. 2, Chap. 6.
28. *Can. Journal*, 1 Jan. 1894.
29. Pentland, pp. 108-109.
30. Lady Pentland, in *Archie Gordon*, p. 3.
31. *Can. Journal*, 20 Jan. 1894.
32. *Ibid.*, 9 Jan. 1894.
33. *Ibid.*, 27 Feb. 1894.
34. *Ibid.*, 28 Feb. 1894.
35. An Ottawa pianist, organist, and music teacher; sister of the poet Archibald Lampman.
36. *Can. Journal*, 13 Jan. 1894.
37. Cf. Florence Hamilton Randal, 'Rideau Hall—Past and Present,' *Canadian Magazine*, vol. 12 (1898-9), pp. 155-156.
38. In *More Cracks*, pp. 101-108.
39. D.P.W. Rep., 1897.
40. Cf. *Can. Journal*, p. xxvi.
41. R. MacGregor Dawson, *William Lyon Mackenzie King, a Political Biography, 1874-1923* (Toronto, 1958), pp. 40-41.
42. *Can. Journal*, 15 March 1894.
43. Cf. *Can. Journal*, p. xxx.
44. *Ibid.*, 5 May 1894.
45. *Ibid.*, 7 May 1894.
46. *Ibid.*, 1 May 1894.
47. *Ibid.*, 10 Aug. 1894.
48. *Ibid.*, 16 Aug. 1894.
49. *Ibid.*, 9 Sept. 1894.
50. *Ibid.*, 7 Nov. 1894.
51. *Ibid.*, 28 [27] Nov. 1894.
52. *Ibid.*, 2 Dec. 1894.
53. *Ibid.*, 11 [12] Dec. 1894.
54. *Ibid.*, 13 Feb. 1895. Two studies of Queen Victoria, made at Windsor by F. M. Bell-Smith, are in the National Gallery of Canada (Accession Nos. 6510, 6930).
55. *Ibid.*, 29 March 1895.
56. *Ibid.*, 9 Feb. 1895.
57. *Ibid.*, 25 Feb. 1895.
58. *Ibid.*, 6 March 1895.
59. *More Cracks*, p. 294; Christopher Hussey, *Tait McKenzie, a Sculptor of Youth* (London, 1929), p. 9.
60. And other poets; see *Can. Journal*, 17 May 1895.
61. *Can Journal*, 17 July 1895.
62. *Ibid.*, 18 July 1895.
63. *Ibid.*, 20 [19] Aug. 1895. I am indebted to Mr Colin Graham, director of the Art Gallery of Victoria, for the information that Lady Aberdeen's 'two Miss Carrs' could only have been Emily Carr's elder sisters.
64. *Ibid.*, 22 [21] Aug. 1895.
65. *Ibid.*, 5 and 8 Jan. 1896, and other entries.
66. *Ibid.*, 2 Jan. 1896.
67. *Ibid.*, 7 Jan. 1896.
68. *Ibid.*, 21 April 1896. The portrait is reproduced in colour in *Archie Gordon*, following p. 43.
69. *Ibid.*, 22 Feb. 1896.
70. *Ibid.*, 5 March 1896; *House of Commons Debates*, 3 March 1896 (pp. 2736-2759).
71. Captain John Sinclair (1860-1925) married Lady Marjorie Gordon in 1904 and was raised to the peerage as Baron Pentland in 1909.
72. *Can. Journal*, 22 April 1896; *We Twa*, vol. 2, Chap. 9.
73. *Can. Journal*, 2 and 9 May 1896.
74. *Ibid.*, 7 June 1896.
75. For the views of Conservatives on Lord Aberdeen, especially those of the Tuppers, see L. C. Clark, 'The Conservative Party in the 1890's', C.H.A., *Report*, 1961, pp. 58-74.
76. *Can. Journal*, 4 July 1896.
77. *Ibid.*, 12 Aug. 1896.
78. D.P.W. Rec., Register, Rideau Hall, Jan. 1897.
79. *Can. Journal*, 31 Jan. 1897.
80. *Ibid.*
81. *Ibid.*, 27 Feb. 1897.
82. *Ibid.*, 9 May 1897.
83. *Ibid.*, 7 Sept. 1897.
84. *Ibid.*, 22 Oct. 1897.
85. *Ibid.*, 30 Oct. 1897, and pp. xxx-xxxii. Alfred Worcester (1855-1951) was founder of the Waltham Training Home for Nurses, Waltham, Massachusetts, professor of hygiene at Harvard, 1925-35, and author of books on nursing and hygiene.
86. *Can. Journal*, 7 Nov. 1897.
87. *Ibid.*, 24 Nov. 1897.
88. *Ibid.*, 24 Nov. and 8 Dec. 1897. For both these meetings, see Alfred Worcester, *Nurses and Nursing* (Cambridge, Mass., 1927), quoted in *Can. Journal*, pp. xxxi-xxxii.
89. P.A.C. (microfilm), Minto Papers, Minto to Arthur Elliot, 25 Dec. 1898.
90. *Book of the Victorian Era Ball* (Toronto, 1898); *Can. Journal*, 8 Dec. 1897.
91. *Can. Journal*, Feb.-July 1898 (p. 452).
92. *Ibid.* (p. 452).
93. Randal, 'Rideau Hall—Past and Present,' pp. 154-155.
94. *Can. Journal*, Feb.-July 1898 (p. 456).
95. *We Twa*, vol. 2, p. 87.
96. *Can. Journal*, 19 Nov. 1898 (p. 478).
97. *Ibid.*, 19 Nov. 1898 (pp. 478-479). At this time Lord Aberdeen was advocating reform of the Civil Service by the introduction of examinations.
98. P.A.C., Aberdeen Papers, vol. 5 (Departure from Canada).
99. *Can. Journal*, 19 Nov. 1898 (p. 472).
100. Minto Papers, Minto to Joseph Chamberlain, 20 Aug. 1899.
101. Lady Pentland, in *Archie Gordon*, pp. 29-31.
102. Pentland, p. 212.
103. *Ibid.*, p. 236.

V

A NEW CENTURY

1. Speech, Ottawa, 27 Sept. 1911, in Lord Grey, *Speeches in September and October 1911 and January 1912* (Ottawa, 1912) [*Speeches*], p. 5.
2. John Buchan, *Lord Minto, a Memoir* (London, 1924) [Buchan]; *D.N.B.*, 1912-1921, pp. 172-174; F. H. Underhill, 'Lord Minto on his Governor Generalship,' *C.H.R.*, vol. 40 (1959), pp. 121-131.
3. Quoted in Buchan, p. 83.
4. Lady Minto in Countess of Oxford and Asquith, *Myself when Young, by Famous Women of To-day* (London, 1938) [*Myself when Young*], p. 234; cf. Buchan, p. 117.
5. For a rhyme containing the words 'Wooden Governors' see a cutting from the *Daily Chronicle* for 8 Nov. 1902 in Minto Papers; see also O. D. Skelton, *Life and Letters of Sir Wilfrid Laurier* (Toronto, 1921), vol. 2, pp. 85-86.
6. J. W. Dafoe, *Sir Wilfrid Laurier*, quoted in H. P. Gundy, 'Sir Wilfrid Laurier and Lord Minto,' *C.H.A.*, *Report*, 1952, p. 28; see also Buchan, p. 123ff.
7. In Buchan, p. 179.
8. Gundy, 'Sir Wilfrid Laurier and Lord Minto,' *op. cit.*
9. Major (later Major-General) Lawrence Drummond (1861- ?) was A.D.C. to General Hutton, 1898-9, and Military Secretary to Lord Minto, 1898-1900. He served in the South African War and the First World War.
10. Captain (later Major-Gen. Sir) Arthur Clive Bell (1871- ?) was A.D.C. to Lord Minto 1900-4; he went with the Canadian Contingent to the South African War and served in the First World War.
11. Captain Harry Graham (1874- ?), Coldstream Guards, was A.D.C. to Lord Minto, 1898-1900, and served in South Africa, 1900-2.
12. Minto Papers, Minto to Arthur Elliot, 26 Feb. 1899.
13. Aberdeen Papers, Martin Griffin to Lady Aberdeen, 24 Jan. 1899.
14. *Ibid.*
15. *Ibid.*, Griffin to Lady Aberdeen, 8 May 1900; see also correspondence between Sir Wilfrid and Lady Laurier and Lady Aberdeen.
16. *Ibid.*, Lady Minto to Lady Aberdeen, 19 Sept. 1898.
17. D.P.W. Rep., 1899; 1900; see also Aberdeen Papers, Minto to Aberdeen, 19 Sept. 1898.
18. Minto Papers, Minto to W. S. Fielding, 27 July 1899; Minto to A. Gobeil, 27 July 1899.
19. *Ibid.*, Minto to Fielding, 27 July 1899.
20. Aberdeen Papers, Lady Minto to Lady Aberdeen, 7 Sept. 1898.
21. *Myself when Young*, p. 252.
22. An early book on hockey is included in the Minto Papers.
23. Minto Papers, Minto to Sir Louis Davies, 4 Feb. 1904; *Myself when Young*, p. 254.
24. Buchan, pp. 190-191.
25. Minto Papers, Minto to Arthur Elliot, 20 May 1903; see also Buchan, pp. 167 ff.
26. Gundy, 'Sir Wilfrid Laurier and Lord Minto,' p. 33.
27. See Buchan, pp. 144-149.
28. Memorandum from Minto, Jan. 1900, in Gundy, 'Sir Wilfrid Laurier and Lord Minto,' p. 33.
29. Underhill, 'Lord Minto on his Governor Generalship,' p. 131; Buchan, p. 181; Minto Papers, Minto to Arthur Elliot, 20 May 1903; *Myself when Young*, p. 255.
30. Minto Papers, Minto to Laurier, 1 May 1900.
31. *Ibid.*, *Across Canada to the Klondyke, being the Journal of a Ten Thousand Mile Tour through the "Great West" (July 19th to October 13th 1900 by 'Col: D. Streamer'* (MS); see also *Myself when Young*, pp. 237-245; Buchan, pp. 173-178.
32. Including Edward Farman, a footman, whose daughters in Ottawa have supplied some of the illustrations for this chapter.
33. Minto Papers, 'Across Canada to the Klondyke,' p. 2.
34. *Ibid.*, Minto to Arthur Elliot, 19 Oct. 1900.
35. *Ibid.*, Minto to Arthur Elliot, 25 Nov. 1900; Minto to Laurier, 16 Jan. 1903.
36. Quoted in Underhill, 'Lord Minto on his Governor Generalship,' pp. 130-131; see also Lady Minto, in *National Review* (March 1905), quoted in Buchan, pp. 202-203.
37. Minto Papers, Minto to Arthur Elliot, 31 July 1900.
38. *Ibid.;* cf. Minto to William Mulock, 17 July 1900.
39. *Ibid.*, Minto to Laurier, 29 Jan. 1901; Buchan, pp. 183-184.
40. Captain (later Lt.-Gen. Sir) Stanley Maude (1864-1917): see *D.N.B.*, 1912-1921, pp. 372-374.
41. R. MacGregor Dawson, *William Lyon Mackenzie King* (Toronto, 1958), pp. 127-128, 171-172.
42. Sir Joseph Pope, *The Tour of . . . the Duke and Duchess of Cornwall and York* (Ottawa, 1903) [Pope].
43. In 1900: see Minto Papers, Minto to Arthur Elliot, 13 March 1900.
44. Pope, p. 28; see also pp. 317-318.
45. Minto Papers, Minto to Arthur Elliot, 3 Nov. 1901.
46. D.P.W. Rep., 1901.
47. Pope, p. 44.
48. James Pope-Hennessey, *Queen Mary* (London, 1959), pp. 368-369.
49. Minto Papers, E. S. Maude to Minto [July] 1901.
50. *Ibid.*, Minto to Arthur Elliot, 3 Nov. 1901; Minto to Edward VII, in Buchan, p. 186.
51. Pope, p. 72.
52. Minto Papers, Minto to Lord Wenlock, 6 June 1901 ff.; Minto to Edward VII, in Buchan, p. 186.
53. Minto to Edward VII, in Buchan, p. 186.
54. Cf. Pope, pp. 55, 63; Pope-Hennessey, *Queen Mary*, p. 369.
55. Minto Papers, Lord Grey to Minto, 25 June 1902.
56. Buchan, p. 162; cf. Minto Papers, Minto to Arthur Elliot, 14 Dec. 1902.
57. Minto Papers, Minto to Arthur Elliot, 22 Nov. 1902.
58. *Ibid.*, Minto to Arthur Elliot, 2 Nov. 1902; Buchan, pp. 195-196.
59. *Myself when Young*, p. 252; Buchan, p. 183.
60. Minto Papers, Minto to Laurier, 18 May 1903; Minto to Arthur Elliot, 20 May 1903; Buchan, p. 200.
61. Minto Papers, Minto to Robert Harris, 15 April 1903.
62. *Ibid.*, Minto to Arthur Elliot, 20 May 1903.
63. See Buchan, pp. 150-152; Gundy, 'Sir Wilfrid Laurier and Lord Minto,' p. 36.
64. Minto Papers, Minto to Arthur Elliot, 5 July 1903.
65. *Ibid.*, Minto to Joseph Chamberlain, 17 July 1903.
66. *Ibid.*, Minto to Laurier, 19 Jan. 1904; Buchan, pp. 187-188.
67. Minto Papers, Minto to Arthur Elliot, 2 Jan. 1904; cf. P.A.C. (partly photostat), Grey Papers, Grey to Laurier, 14 Feb. 1905.
68. Minto Papers, Minto to Sir Henry Elliot, 24 April 1904; Buchan, p. 183.
69. Gundy, 'Sir Wilfrid Laurier and Lord Minto,' p. 38.
70. See also Lady Minto, *India, Minto & Morley* (London, 1935).
71. See *Addresses to His Excellency Earl Grey . . . and his Speeches in Reply* (Ottawa, 1908) [*Addresses*].
72. P.A.C. (microfilm), Goldwin Smith Papers, John Morley to Goldwin Smith, 28 April 1905.
73. *D.N.B.*, 1912-1921, pp. 227-228; Harold Begie, *Albert 4th Earl Grey; a Last Word* (London, 1917); Interview with Lady Evelyn Jones, 1962.
74. Grey Papers, Edward VII to Grey, 25 Aug. 1904.
75. Quoted in *D.N.B.*, 1912-1921, p. 228.
76. Minto Papers, Grey to Minto, 15 Oct. 1904; see also Grey Papers, Correspondence with Laurier commencing July 1905.